Making Connections

Making Connections

Mother-Daughter Travel Adventures

Edited by Wendy Knight

Seal Press

Making Connections: Mother-Daughter Travel Adventures

Published by Seal Press
An Imprint of Avalon Publishing Group, Incorporated
161 William St., 16th Floor
New York, NY 10038

Library of Congress Cataloging-in-Publication Data is available.

ISBN 1-58005-087-5

9 8 7 6 5 4 3 2 1

Designed by Shona McCarthy
Printed in the United States of America
Distributed by Publishers Group West

Contents

Distance

Release

Ritual

Mortality

For my mother, Mary, with whom
I've shared many of life's adventures

and

For my daughter, Alex, my delightful voice of reason

Go ahead, push your luck
find out how much love
the world can hold.

—Dar Williams

Introduction

This book germinated in the embers of a wildfire.

Three summers ago, I had arranged to spend a week rafting and camping along the Salmon River in Idaho with my thirteen-year-old daughter, Alex.

"Fires Force Salmon River Closure" read the morning headlines in the *Idaho Statesman* the day before our scheduled launch on the Main Salmon. Disappointed that we were forced to abandon the raft trip, I suggested we take a short hike in the Sawtooth Mountains where the air was clear before we headed back to Sun Valley. Studying the topographical map, I found a gentle trail to Titus Lake, just south of 8,700-foot Galena Summit.

An hour later, we came upon a bowl of emerald green rimmed with Douglas firs and Ponderosa pines. As we rested on the shore, two household cats absorbing the sun's heat, I noticed a huge white cloud cresting the hill about a mile west of the lake. While Alex chattered, I cautiously watched the cloud. The cotton ball had turned dense and gray and appeared to be spreading up and out across the ridge, a swath of soiled cloth unfurling against a blue sky.

Not wanting to alarm my daughter, I nonchalantly announced it was time to leave and we packed up and moved toward the trail. A couple from across the lake bolted past. I glanced behind for a status of the darkening cloud and, to my horror, saw huge flames swaying and thrusting up in angry bursts beyond the hills.

"Alex," I said calmly, pointing to the shades of amber and scarlet dancing in the sky, "we've gotta run."

Her face went pale and her eyes widened. Within seconds, the sky turned dark and heavy. Off to the left, where the fire was flanking us, the air felt like an oven door had been left open.

"Mom, I can feel the heat," Alex cried, as we ran toward the trailhead.

At times, we appeared to be racing straight into the darkness, swirls of orange and gray circling above the treetops. When we sighted the road ahead, our relief was palpable and we shed our fear like a snake's skin. Silently, we walked across the deserted road, the eerie calm and smoke-filled sky an apocalyptic scene from a movie set.

"I don't want to hike anymore," Alex said, crawling into the safety of our vehicle.

I wasn't sure if she meant on this vacation or ever, but I couldn't blame her either way.

Within hours we laughed about our near-tragedy in the forest as we envisioned her reply when asked, "So what did *you* do this summer?" And when we gathered for the holidays later that year and the inevitable "remember when" tales began, my aunts assured Alex what great stories she'd have when she reached my age, or theirs, if she lived that long, of course, they joked. We all chuckled, but I knew it wasn't funny, the potential danger I placed her in, my beloved child.

Aside from captivating story-telling material, our experience in the Sawtooths illuminated Alex's and my divergent perspectives on traveling in the outdoors. She's a quiet, cautious child who would rather read a book, perhaps even clean her room, than walk in the woods. And while we enjoy our many travels, it's a struggle to engage her in any prolonged outdoor pursuit. Convinced of nature's potent wisdom, I often resort to bribes or coercion to lure her into the wilderness.

Getting caught in a forest fire forced me to question my responsibilities as an adventurous parent. Do I personally threaten her safety when I take her rafting down the Colorado River or hiking in the Tetons? At what point does adventure become recklessness?

More fundamentally, I began to look squarely at my internal irony: I joyfully and enthusiastically embrace motherhood, yet I routinely seek to move freely about the world unencumbered by maternal accountability. I relish the unexpected encounters with the natural world and the momentary connections with people that traveling solo engender. But I want desperately to be grounded, and feel most content when I'm home with Alex. This long-standing dichotomy was dramatically illuminated during my trip to Sudan, a remote, war-torn country I visited against nearly everyone's counsel, and left only because of my daughter.

This collection of twenty-six essays digs deep into the emotional ambivalence of motherhood, confronts the unspoken leash that women unwittingly or intentionally tether to their daughters, and explores the range of complex issues surrounding mothers and daughters—independence, self-worth, approval—in the context of travel.

Travel is a powerful elixir. We use it to escape, and to come home. Adventure travel, in particularly, can strip us of our familial roles or corner us into them. Who takes the lead in uncertain or dangerous circumstances? Acquiesces? Seeks a truce? Pushes forward? Retreats to denial? Assigns blame? Fosters resentments? The psychological terrain mothers and daughters navigate is infinitely more challenging than the physical obstacles we encounter on terra firma.

The authors of these stories transport us to the sacred mountains of Peru, the deserts of Afghanistan, and to the verdant hills of Vietnam, but more importantly they take us through the irreconcilable rifts, clumsy reconnections, profound admiration, and durable bonds between mothers and daughters.

The book is divided into sections that span the emotional arc of motherhood. The essays in "Anew" reveal the apprehension of an impending birth or a fresh start. Moms and daughters wrestle with the complexities of opposing personas in "Identity"and begin to see each other differently under the halogen of unfamiliar circumstances in "Risk." In "Distance" and "Release" women struggle with estrangement and attempted reconciliation, then with the liberation of finally letting go. The essays in "Ritual" honor the subtle declarations of love found in small moments and confront the advancing years of mothers in "Mortality." And finally, the essays in "Home" illustrate the serenity that comes from finding one's place in the world.

Ultimately, this book is about the enduring strength of love—not a fictionalized or vapid interpretation of motherly care—but the truly inspiring moments of acceptance and forgiveness that mothers and daughters bestow on each other, or find for themselves.

Making Connections

Anew

Waiting

by Molly Ambrecht Absolon

Mt. Baker floats like a cloud above the shoreline. The white snow of its glaciers has been yellowed to the color of old lace by smog along the horizon. It looks like a perfect day for summiting. The skies are clear and the wind calm. I imagine rope teams of climbers snaking their way through crevasse fields on their way to and from the uppermost reaches of the mountain. If I close my eyes, I can see the glittering ice and hear the crunch of the snow beneath my plastic boots. The sun burns the back of my neck and cracks my lips as if I were there.

Though I've never climbed Mt. Baker, I've ascended other peaks. On these expeditions, we'd switch to a night schedule to avoid the heat of the afternoon sun reflecting off the glaciers. By noon we'd have a perimeter probed and wanded, and our sleeping bags draped over the outside of the tent to keep out the sun. Inside we'd try to sleep, read, or count the squares in the weave of the rip-stop nylon dome over our heads, waiting for dinner, waiting for a storm to end, waiting for sleep, waiting to move up again.

Waiting

I'm waiting now, but not to climb. Across Puget Sound, Mt. Baker is an icon on the horizon that keeps pulling my eyes up, up to the summit, taunting me with my past. I'm seven months pregnant and my climbing harness no longer fits. In front of me, on a narrow, gray strip of beach, the drama of my future plays itself out.

Three little girls run up and down on the sand keeping just out of reach of the gently slapping waves, their bellies high and round and their sand-covered buttocks peeking out from beneath purple, pink, and yellow bathing suits. A little boy builds a sandcastle, then stomps it flat and starts anew. Women, burdened by duffels hanging off their shoulders, coolers in their hands, and mats rolled up beneath their arms, walk past trailed by toddlers asking questions in high-pitched voices or crying because of the hot sand under their feet. I can only guess what these women have brought to the beach to feed, clothe, and entertain their kids. What I know is how to coil a rope, how to climb the cracks of a cliff, how to pack for a three-week expedition.

When we introduce ourselves to strangers, we don't ask what makes the other laugh or lie awake at night. Instead, we open the conversation with "What do you do?" As if the answer defines who we really are: investment banker, doctor, teacher, lawyer. I've used different labels, but labels nonetheless. I am a climber, a mountaineer, a skier, someone who makes her living taking people out into the wilderness. I had grown to believe those labels defined who I really was. I never had time for children, never had time for anything but the next workout, the next ascent, the next expedition. My body was an instrument I tuned for a symphony of motion. I was in control. I was in motion. Now she, this being inside me, is in control and forcing me to be still.

My belly has grown, swelling with defiant pride, thrusting itself in front of me as my daughter announces her imminent arrival. Her boldness seems almost obscene to me. I want to hide away in my house, cower behind windows draped with blankets to keep out the afternoon sun. Waiting. Waiting until I get my body back, until I come back. But I am not coming back, not the way I was.

I have never been overtly maternal. There was no emotional clock ticking for motherhood. Internally, I recoiled when someone would shove a baby in my arms asking me if I wanted to hold him or her. While I didn't, it felt unnatural not to. Then suddenly I was in my mid-thirties. The climbing, the trips, the adrenaline seemed repetitive. I began to wonder if I was missing something, and if maybe that something was a child.

A thin sweeping crack splits the face of Belle Fourche Buttress on Devil's Tower. The crack is white from the hands of thousands of climbers. My hands are white, chalked, ready. I slot a stopper into the groove, pulling down on the wire stem to make sure it is secure before clipping in the climbing rope. I reach up and feel the insides of the crack, the pinches and flares and uneven crystals, searching for a spot where my fingers will lock and allow me to move up off the ledge.

Part of me wants to turn away, to stop the fear that gnaws at me, to quiet the voice that keeps screaming, "You can't do this, it's too hard, you aren't good enough."

But moving up and leaving the ledge is what made me feel good enough. It's what made me feel. So I blocked out the voices and climbed. I climbed in the mountains, in the canyons. I climbed frozen waterfalls, glaciers, cliffs, and snow-slopes. The rope bound me to my husband, to my friends, to my community, to the land. The rope took me to places where peregrine falcons shrieked at my trespass and fairy gardens of saxifrage and moss campion softened the sterility of the stone. It tied me to an identity and told me who I was. But now, that rope has been cut. I don't know when I will climb another mountain, when my husband and I will tie into a rope together. I don't know who I am.

As I sit with my sister here on Puget Sound, people ask her about climbing and me about my pregnancy. I want to scream, "Wait, I know more about climbing than I do about children. I taught my sister how to climb! All I've done is read books about children."

But my pregnancy has taken over. I wasn't prepared for that. I didn't expect my belly to swallow me whole.

We weren't even sure we were fertile. Once my husband and I decided that we did want to have a child, it took two years for me to conceive and during those months of taking temperatures and charting mucus cycles, months of businesslike, on-time sex, I refused to think or talk about children. I refused to consider what we would do if nothing happened or what we would do if it did. I thought I knew I wanted a child but what that really meant I wasn't sure. I wanted a family. I wanted my life to be about more than my latest climb or mountaineering epic. I did not want to be alone in my old age. So I guessed that meant I wanted a baby.

In January, I went in for a routine check-up. My period was late, but only by a week or so, and I'd had cramps so I was sure that it would come any day. The nurse asked me if I wanted to do a pregnancy test, just to see. I said yes, just to see. Then she showed me the red line across the strip of paper. I couldn't see. Her smile told me: Positive. The test was positive. Just to see, just in case. Mother. I am going to become a mother.

The label "mother" had always been a conversation stopper in my crowd. We're the twenty- to forty-something childless outdoorsy wanderers whose cars sport bike racks, ski racks, boat racks, and built-in mattresses. We say "that's nice" when someone gets pregnant, and then never see them again as their adventures change from two weeks of mountaineering in the Alaska Range to two weeks at the beach with the grandparents.

I like my life. It's exciting, romantic, and full of adventure. I guess it also makes me feel cool. I don't think I've ever really felt mothering was cool. I watch the women on the beach—burdened with armloads of junk—with dread. My life has always been fast, spontaneous, light. Do I really want to let go of that? Have I made a terrible mistake?

People say that you don't feel you've given anything up once the child is born, that you are so in love with your baby your desires change. I don't know what those new desires will be. I don't know what I will dream about or what I will dread. I do know I feel an incredible sense of joy when my daughter twists and turns inside my womb. But right now, at seven months, I'm in between two worlds, one I know and one I don't. I have always hated silences. I squirm and long for someone to say something, anything, to fill the empty space. Now I'm in that empty space, waiting.

Wuhu Diary

by Emily Prager

When her adopted daughter, Lulu, was four, Emily Prager took her back to Wuhu, the town in southern China where Lulu was born and lived in an orphanage as an infant. This excerpt from Wuhu Diary, *Prager's account of their two-month journey, describes their attempt to visit the orphanage.*

I am sick. I stagger into the bathroom and hunt out the adult antibiotics I brought from the United States. As I'm downing them, there's a knock at the door and I open it to three giggling, very shy Chinese girls in their late teens. One of them is Caroline.

I ask her if she wouldn't mind coming back after lunch and taking us around then. This seems to please them all and they rush off.

While I rest, LuLu watches a kids' show on television, and just before we leave for lunch—lo and behold!—the English-language news comes on again. We are rushing out, but I linger to catch the highlights. The commentator, a matter-of-fact woman in her mid-thirties whom I dub Barbara Walters Wong, announces that the Chinese embassy in Belgrade has been bombed and that investigations are under way to see who is responsible. There is a possibility, she says somberly, that the United States may have done it.

That's impossible, I think. Clinton would never do that. I shut off the TV as Wong begins to talk about preparations in Beijing for celebrations of the May 4th Movement.

The May 4th Movement was the first mass demonstration in Chinese history. In 1919, after World War I, five thousand Chinese university students protested the Versailles Conference mandate assigning Kiaochow in Shantung Province to Japan. Their outrage led to a nationwide boycott of Japanese goods and a whirlwind of intellectual discussion, which led to attacks on Confucianism. Marxist and democratic principles were taken up, and modern ideas (like women participating in politics) were espoused. Out of this foment came the founding of both the Chinese Communist party and the Kuomintang.

LuLu and I trot up the leafy roadway on the other side of Building Two to the restaurant, or Canting, as I see it is misspelled. We pass by Building Three and then turn right to climb a very steep set of elderly stone stairs. These stairs remind me of the ones I have seen in the Forbidden City and are separated in the middle by a smooth stretch of stone so heavy that carts can be pushed up them. It is evidently a very ancient construction design.

We go through glass doors into the restaurant and a hostess greets us as we enter. She looks like a model and stands about six feet tall, wearing a floor-length cheongsam slit quite high on the sides.

The Chinese girls we have seen so far are of a pretty good height, many of them very tall. The days of short Chinese are clearly over. LuLu has always been tall for her age. Right now she's in the eightieth percentile for American boys, although the pediatrician told me that Asian kids sometimes shoot up early, and without seeing her genetics, he couldn't tell how tall she would actually be.

Funnily enough, that is something that really irks me. While I don't mind having my authenticity as a parent constantly questioned, I do mind not knowing how tall my daughter is going to be. I have a health record at home that says LuLu was 7.7 pounds, twenty-three inches, at birth. I think they got it wrong. She was only eleven pounds when I got her at seven months, and twenty-three inches at birth would probably mean she'd end up six feet five inches tall.

Right inside the doors of the restaurant are two banks of fish tanks full of live lobsters, eels, and fish. LuLu loves these, of course, and spends time checking on the inhabitants while I take one of the vast number of empty, white-tableclothed tables. I try not to feel self-conscious.

After a wonderful lunch, I feel better. We go down to the huge pine tree in the main plaza to meet Caroline. In my purse I have the addresses of the places where LuLu and Francesca were found. Since I don't feel so well, I figure we will take a taxi ride to locate these places and photograph them. As far as LuLu and Caroline are concerned, we will simply be sight-seeing.

Caroline is twenty years old and about five feet seven. She comes from Ma'anshan and is studying to be a teacher. She wears the characteristic fashion of the Wuhu college girl, a cotton ankle-length jumper dress, very simply and geometrically cut, which gathers with a pull string at the neck. Underneath is a white cotton long-sleeved blouse. Over all, she carries a cloth backpack. The whole outfit, which in America would look trendy, in China resembles a modern version of ancient Chinese women's dress as seen in scroll painting. Her shoes are black and platformed. She has a plain, sensible, affectless face.

We walk out to the taxi queue and I choose the one woman driver, an energetic, no-nonsense gal with a ponytail who looks like a dancer in a Broadway musical about China. Her name is Miss Swallow. I bundle LuLu and Caroline into the backseat of her cab.

I show Caroline the address of the place LuLu was found and tell her I want to go there. She and Miss Swallow confer.

LuLu leans back and stares out the window at her town. The taxi goes down GengXing to Laodong Road, turns left, goes up to Sun Yat-sen, takes a left spoke, and swings around Jing Hu Lake. As we do this, I notice swan and duck boats in the water for rent, the kind you paddle with your feet, just as they have in Boston. In fact, Wuhu in some indescribable way reminds me of Boston. I'm not sure what it is—the size, the formality, the lake, or what.

The lake is divided by a picturesque round-backed little bridge that looks so like the bridge that's a clue in *Big Bird in China* that LuLu gets all excited when she sees it. The taxi weaves around the rubble and half-built skyscrapers at this end of the lake, and comes to a halt before a modern bridge over a small canal that feeds into the Yangtze River. You can just see a little sliver of it in the distance.

On our side of the bridge is the department store Xin Bei, fronted by rubble. On the other side of the bridge lies the rest of Wuhu, which has not been so rebuilt and, I can see, looks kind of gray and grim.

"Here," Miss Swallow tells Caroline, who tells me, and she stops the car. "Here is the Qing Yi Jiang Canal."

"Here?" I echo hollowly.

LuLu stays in the car and plays with Caroline while I jump out, taking my camera.

Here? My daughter, the child I adore so much, was abandoned here? Here.

Fortunately, there is not much traffic on the bridge, which allows me to run up on it and just stand there and stare. I drop my eyes down from the heights of the bridge to the little canal, where a number of wooden houseboats are parked. Was she born on one of those houseboats? Did they sail up the canal to the bridge to leave her here?

I look up. In the distance, a little pagoda rises like a lighthouse, facing the river. It stands like a tiny beacon at the end of the canal. There are pictures of it in Building Two. It is the one tourist attraction in Wuhu.

The bridge I am standing on is industrial and modern. The people of the city are crossing on bicycles and in trucks, and it's a busy place.

But I find it totally surreal. I hadn't expected the place to look so . . . what? So urban, so twentieth-century. I don't know what I thought: that it would be more ancient-looking somehow? Just as I thought that Wuhu would be more like a village, with a dusty main street.

But no, Wuhu is a city and LuLu's bridge is modern. Was it this way four years ago? I ask Miss Swallow. The bridge was the same.

I walk to the other end of the bridge and look down at some of the older houses. Yes, it was definitely slummier at one time. Was it by this ramshackle, redbrick house at the bridge's corner that she was left? I imagine my baby as she was, lying there, wrapped up and crying—her familiar cry that I've known so well for these last four years, that I could pick out of a crowd of crying babies.

I remember when she first came home, there was a dog that barked in the courtyard in back of our brownstone. It was the only thing that made her cry loudly and fearfully, and I always thought, when she was out there on the street, had a dog bark scared her?

But there are no dogs in Wuhu, and when she cried out, she wasn't on a dusty village street with dogs running about, as I once fantasized. She was lying right here, in the middle of her city, near this bridge that half of Wuhu crosses every day.

I stare down at the canal. Did her people bring her on a houseboat? Lu, with her love of boats and water? They could have. Did they bring her up out of the houseboat and place her right here?

And how long was she in the street here? They found her at three days old. Was it one day, two days, or all three?

I suddenly realize the importance of this journey we are taking. It is absolutely true that very soon all trace of what we can know of her past will be bulldozed away. Trying to sound very casual, I tell Caroline that we would like to visit the Wuhu Children's Institute. Could we drive there right now? I call it, as she does, "the Welfare," so LuLu will not understand.

"Oh, sure," replies Caroline. "That's easy." And she talks to Miss Swallow, who nods and drives across the bridge into the older part of Wuhu. Miss Swallow weaves the car through what are clearly slums, and now and then stops to ask people directions. "Not many people know the address of Welfare," says Caroline, to explain Miss Swallow's difficulty. "Do you?" I ask.

"Oh, yes. I went on a school trip there," she replies. "What was it like?" I persist.

She bows her head and looks away, knowing LuLu is from there and not wanting to offend. "It was miserable," she says softly.

I slough off this comment as prejudice, since I know that there is a sort of 1950s horror here about orphans, the disabled, and the mentally disabled, all of whom are more or less lumped together. To a Chinese, having no family is the metaphorical equivalent to having no limbs.

I have made the snap decision to drop by the institute just in case we are denied entry through channels. I was always nervous about asking permission, because once you ask, they know you are here and can refuse you. It is my friendship with Leo that has made me go through channels. He is the citizen here, not me.

The officials in Hefei probably aren't in daily contact with the orphanage director in Wuhu; and if they are and there is a problem, I will simply say that, knowing Lu's story, the taxi driver drove us there on her tour before I realized.

Miss Swallow is driving around, turning here and there and asking people. She talks with Caroline as she does so. It seems that the institute has moved recently and the building that it was in was torn down.

So . . . it is not the place LuLu was in as an infant. I digest this slowly. It is nearer to the main part of the city and in better shape, evidently. Okay. I take in this disappointment. She will never see the actual place. Okay.

LuLu does know we are trying to visit "the institute" while in Wuhu, but she doesn't seem to realize that we are on our way there now. I want to see the place first, make sure it is palatable.

Pretty soon, Miss Swallow comes to a halt in a congested area by a railroad track. She points across the street, and we all get out. Lu and I follow Caroline as she crosses the dusty thoroughfare and enters a narrow alley, past a market set up there.

We walk by a live-eel salesman and a live-chicken salesman, and then we come to the live-frog salesman. The man is skinning the bodies of live frogs from the neck down. Lovely. But, strangely, the frogs seem not to mind this and are hopping about quite well, skinless, looking as if they are wearing frog heads. Four-year-old LuLu is fascinated by this and insists on watching the process intently. I can't take it.

I drag her away by the hand and Caroline leads us down the alley, which becomes a street of the very *hutongs* that they are tearing down all over Wuhu: small, dark, one-room shacklike structures built across from one another on a cobblestone street as narrow as two human arm spans.

Along this rather fetid but ancient and picturesque cobblestoned way, there are open stalls selling magazines, candy, some clothing, and food. Presently, we come to a run-down gated compound. Between dirty stone pillars, a metal gate allows me to look in and see a drab courtyard. One grim-looking leafless tree grows in the center of it, mired in a bed of mud. A long, low wooden building hunches down behind it, all shut up tight. There is no evidence of little children anywhere and nothing green.

I crane my neck and see an archway that leads to another, interior court. In there, a disheveled and rather grimy adolescent girl is sitting silently, lost in reverie.

A gnarled old man at the gate, the security guard, tells Caroline that since it is Saturday, there are no officials about and we cannot come in. As he is saying this, suddenly, LuLu drops my hand, squeezes by him, and runs as fast as she can through the courtyard and beyond into the interior court. Once there, she stands motionless, looking all around her, finally fixing on the adolescent girl. I can almost see the energy popping out of her tense little body.

It happens so fast that for a minute I'm stunned. Then, before I can stop him, the old man runs after LuLu, shouting harshly. I rush in the gate after him to get her, but LuLu doesn't stop or come out; she runs farther into the interior courtyard. Again, she stands her ground and looks all around her.

The adolescent girl, who I now realize is retarded in some way, becomes scared and cringes as the old man harshly shoos her away to somewhere inside. Lu watches this for a moment and then speeds back toward me.

Tears course down my cheeks. Someplace less congenial than this is where my daughter spent the first seven months of her infant life. And it is not that it's so awful or even that I didn't expect it to be minimal, or even harsh. It's that I am really looking at it. It's not a fantasy. And I can't help it: I'm devastated.

"Pick me up, Mama," says LuLu, which I do as fast as I can. I hold her close, explaining that the old man is afraid and not to worry. She rests on my neck and hugs me back. I try to stop my tears, but they are streaming down my face.

Caroline and the old man assume that I am crying because we are not allowed to go in. The old man apologizes profusely now but says I must go to the police station to get a permit with a stamp, and then I'll be allowed in. Clearly he is shaken up. He asks us to leave.

I walk out through the gate silently, carrying LuLu.

As soon as we are beyond it, LuLu asks to get down. She has seen some children her age, with whom she now goes off to play. The kids accept her instantly and they invent a game, jumping off some little stairs and poring over the cobblestones, looking for spiders.

I stand there composing myself, thinking frantically how to make this all right for LuLu. I am in shock. This was definitely not the return I had envisioned. I have no idea how much LuLu has really understood of what has gone on. But somehow, without my saying so, she certainly seemed to understand that this was a place she should take a good look at, and no one was going to stop her. Perhaps she even intuited that this was the institute.

Suddenly, she appears back at my side and tugs on my shirt. I look down at her and she stretches her little hand up to me. Clenched in her little fingers is a bouquet of the tiniest red flowers I've ever seen. She hands them to me and her little almond-shaped eyes look into mine so lovingly. Then she quickly scampers away to play with the children.

I am so moved by her gesture that I can barely stand it. I go over to where she is playing and take my little girl's hand and kiss it. I look around on the dusty, squalid street. There are certainly no flowers anywhere around, anywhere at all. I can't imagine where she found them.

"Thank you, LuLu," I manage. "Thank you so much." She gets up from playing and walks back by my side, down the cobblestoned street.

"I'm sorry, LuLu," I say, leaning down to her. "Did the man upset you? He was afraid."

"Where are the children?" she asks. So she knew.

"I think they were inside," I reply. "Maybe napping."

"I want to see inside," she says.

"All right," I say. "Okay. We will try. We will go back next week and take some toys to the children. Would you like that?"

"Yes," she replies matter-of-factly. "Yes. I would."

Next to me, Caroline is still horrified that her countryman has made the foreign woman cry. To console me, she buys me a piece of special Wuhu candy from a stall.

We get back to the taxi and I hand Caroline the address of the police station where Janine's daughter, Francesca, was found. As we drive off, LuLu falls to sleep, lulled by the sound of the car motor.

We drive over the railroad tracks and down a rather busy avenue crammed with pedicabs (bicycle rickshaws), red taxis, people on bicycles, and the occasional truck. We pass a Catholic church with a big stone angel in front. I make Miss Swallow stop, and I get out and take pictures of the environs and the big angel for Janine.

After some maneuvering through crowds of bicycles, our taxi stops at a rather dreary-looking police station building. Near here is where Francesca was found. The avenue turns out to be another end of Laodong Road. To make the place look a bit more festive, I take a picture of a man selling red cloth from a little glass stall, leaving the police station in the background.

But once again, I am staggered. This is a busy avenue. I try to imagine a little bundle containing Lu's friend Francesca lying here near the chaos. I then switch to LuLu and Francesca riding together in Francesca's Barbie jeep out on her lawn last summer. It's unbelievable. And what I realize is that their lives now are so vastly different from what they would have been that it is not that these girls are "lucky," as people are wont to say; no, their collective fate is some sort of miracle.

I get back in the car and let Miss Swallow take us on her tour. She drives us far out of town to "the new urban area," as Caroline calls it, a stretch of green farmland where enormous industrial factories, many of them German, have been built. Caroline and Miss Swallow are both very proud of this complex.

There is nothing else here but the buildings, unkempt grass, and rice paddies. It has the empty look of Mayan temple complexes overgrown by the jungles of Guatemala. There's no city out here, no people visible. I guess this is where the foreign businessmen who stay at the hotel go all day. This is the area that will save Anhui from the terrible poverty that has always gripped it.

On the drive back to the hotel, I ask Miss Swallow whether she minds all the old buildings being torn down in Wuhu.

"I can't wait to see them all go," she replies, laughing. Caroline explains that everyone wants light in their apartments and air, and, of course, the rooms are bigger.

Caroline and I make a date to meet the next morning. She will take us to a children's park called the Water Palace. I love that name.

As we disembark at the main plaza, Lu spots TohToh, the doorman on duty, and runs to play with him. She shrieks with joy as he teases her and throws her up in the air. I collapse on the red-carpeted stairs in front of our building and think over what occurred.

I was surprised that Wuhu Children's Institute is such a small facility. Very small. And it was interesting that there were no children outside. I had thought they would be out. Some babies in our group were very tanned from being outside in the sun so much. I had always pictured the babies sitting outside.

I think back to when LuLu handed me the bouquet of tiny flowers. They were as small as pinheads. What was she saying with them? I know only that the expression in her eyes was so wise, it melted my heart.

Deep in my daughter lies a knowledge that I will never have. I have always been aware of this. She has shown it to me through her hyperawareness of who and what is around her and her lightning ability to grasp the relationships between people. She is a little child, yet she trusts herself before me, her own ability to survive before my advice. In this she differs from all birth children I have met. And she is right to. It is she who survived her circumstances, not me. How could she view it any other way?

But I didn't really know the extent of what she knew until the day we visited my mother in the hospital.

It was the week my mother went in for tests. As yet, they had not found her cancer, but she was in terrible shape. I took LuLu with me because I knew it would be one of the last times she could see her grandmother, who was fading quickly.

I had started to prepare LuLu that Grandma would not always be with us, that soon she would die. LuLu asked me what death was, and I explained what different religions believe death to be. I told her about heaven and hell; merging with the cosmos; rebirth and reincarnation; and just disintegrating. She instantly embraced rebirth and reincarnation (as befits a descendant of Buddhists), and decided to believe that. She derived clear comfort from the idea that my mother might be reborn as a baby.

Anyway, I took LuLu to the hospital, and when we arrived, my mother was asleep. She looked pretty ghastly, emaciated and worn out.

I took my mother's hand and held it, and Lu held her other hand. After a few minutes, we left.

When we got home, my stepfather called and I told him that he should prepare himself because I didn't think it would be long for Mom. Ever the optimist, he started to demur. LuLu, then just four, took the phone out of my hand and said in a deep, serious tone I had never heard her use before, "Grandma is going to die, Grandpa. Very soon. I know it. She's going to die soon."

I was startled. I took back the receiver, and my stepfather was silent for several moments. Finally he said, "That was very definite." And for the first time since my mother had become critically ill, he began to deal with it.

Later that evening, I asked LuLu, "Why are you so sure Grandma is going to die? Have you ever seen someone die?"

"Yes," she said without hesitation. "In the orphanage. The mother went to feed the baby, but the baby was dead."

Chills ran down my arms. LuLu had never mentioned the orphanage before, ever. I don't think she had ever uttered the word. And she was not the kind of child who made up fantasies. In fact, she rarely fantasized, which worried me, as if she was, as yet, afraid to leave her present, safe reality. So when she said this, even though I had fed her the idea, I was pretty sure she was not just making up a story.

I knew from what Spence-Chapin told us that in the orphanage, the infants often slept together, five or six to a crib, for company and warmth. This was why, Spence said, some of the babies considered it a punishment to sleep alone. LuLu always refused to. She would cry pitifully in protest, and it was the only thing she cried about. Later, when she started to talk, she told me that she could see no point to sleeping alone at all. Why would anyone want to sleep by themselves, she would ask, when they could snuggle?

So she had probably slept with other babies. I knew from a friend who had visited a large orphanage in 1992 and was among the first to adopt from China, that the sick babies were not, at that time, necessarily separated from the well ones, especially in the poorer facilities.

It was entirely possible that one of the babies in Lu's bed had died in the night and that the nurse—in an infant's mind a mother—had come to feed them in the morning and discovered the child.

Had my daughter lain all night next to another infant who was dying or dead? I don't know. I know only that LuLu was correct in her assessment of my mother. The hospice nurse gave my mother three to six months to live, but she died as Lu prophesied, "very soon," several days later.

I watch LuLu as she plays with TohToh. She seems full of happiness now, running around and hiding from him, chortling with gaiety. Her long black hair streams behind her round baby body as she flees. I dash into the computer room and e-mail Neke and Martha about what happened at the orphanage. I write down Neke's e-mail to LuLu to read to her later. I am very glad to have this means of near instant communication. Martha always reassures me, bless her.

I gather up LuLu and we go to the Canting, where we eat a dinner of dumplings in soup. Again, about fifteen young waitresses are standing around, with only a few people to serve. When we are finished, LuLu goes outside to look for bugs at the edge of the stairs while I pay the check. Twenty yuan is a lot to pay; a typical bill is about ten ($1.25).

When I get out to her, LuLu is chatting with three friendly-looking men whom I will come to know as Mr. Tong, Mr. Wu, and Mr. Tchang, managers, respectively, of the Canting and the hotel. They are all dressed in navy pleated trousers and white shirts, and when they talk among themselves, they are exactly like men of their age in America discussing business, only more relaxed somehow. They laugh a lot.

Mr. Tong is a robust man in his late thirties with black wavy hair and a dimply, round-faced smile. He is the Canting manager. Mr. Wu is in his mid-thirties and very handsome in a tall, Harrison Ford–type way. Mr. Tchang, also in his mid-thirties, is slender, wiry, and intelligent-looking. He is the head manager.

LuLu is laughing and showing them her finds. They are teasing her about her spiders and bugs.

I nod to them and take her down the hill to our building. There is a new attendant on our floor, a strong-looking girl whose name is LingLing. She opens the door for us, and I go in and turn on the TV.

The English-language news is pro-Belgrade, but there is no mention of anything new. Nelson Mandela is visiting Beijing. There are big celebrations going on to commemorate the May 4th Movement. And a ban on learning Mandarin has been lifted in Indonesia. Hearing the news in a Communist country is always like peering out at the world from the other side of the mirror.

As I put LuLu to bed, I see the housemaids have noticed that Lu and I sleep together, and have turned down only one bed. I read to LuLu from *Stuart Little* and she drops effortlessly to sleep, with me following suit soon after.

Naming Our Canyon

by Hannah Nyala

"It's a desert oasis, so it isn't going anywhere. We don't have to hurry. Nothing's on fire."

If I said that once, I said it ten times in the first mile, and for every time I mumbled it aloud I must've thought it forty times more, but it didn't change my six-year-old daughter's mind—or the pace at which her feet hit the ground—one bit. Sam, our young search dog, loped along beside her. I trotted to keep up with them.

"I'm not worried about it going anywhere, Mommy," Ruth finally said impatiently, illustrating the point with both hands as if explaining a very simple matter to a very simple soul, and never decelerating her feet in the least. "But if we get there sooner, then we can be there longer."

Oh. Now why hadn't I thought of that? So much for my plans for a leisurely weekend backpacking trip with my youngest child. Eight miles round-trip in the southern California desert, Cottonwood Springs to Lost Palms Oasis and back, and three days to do it in; girl talk, woman talk, healing, forgiving, bridging the gap that the last two years of living apart had created between us, finding a way to walk toward a future that still looked rather grim.

Ruth had been home only a little more than a week the morning we set out on our hike, and the anguish of the past two years still weighed heavily on both of us. We were technically safe, yet substantively not, especially in the ways that perhaps matter most. Family violence respects no boundaries; carves out no moats about your existence: Ruth and I were home, but her brother Jon was still living with the man who had battered all three of us, and we had no way to change the situation. So although my daughter and I clung to one another and meant it, there was still a chasm of indescribable dimensions between us as we headed toward Lost Palms that morning. My plan was for the camping trip to bring us back together and give us some reasons for continued hope. Such a good plan it was too. So good it probably deserved the vigorous dusting in the soot of reality my daughter was all poised to give it. She slowed down only twice that morning—once for a chuckwalla and once for a rattlesnake. The rest of the time we hustled toward our destination with all the fervor of a small freight train.

Reaching the hill above the oasis in record time, we headed downward at a fast trot. When we got within an untested stone's throw of its tall trees, Ruthie stopped so abruptly I almost bumped into her. Small rocks skittered out from underneath my hiking boots, and I threw both arms out to the side to keep my balance.

Ruth appeared not to notice my difficulties, and I still believe that had to have taken some effort, although she denies it to this day.

"Well, we're here," she said, dropping her small daypack on the ground. "And I'm thirsty."

Perhaps some lingering snittiness about the speed of the journey's first half got stuck in my craw, I don't know, but I replied, one hair shy of testy and with a deadpan face, "Well, technically we aren't really at the oasis till we're under the palms, so maybe we should hurry right on down there before we get a drink."

Ruth looked at me so straight I nearly sneezed. One full second passed, then two, three.

Finally she said, "I'm all hurried out. And besides, you said it wasn't going anywhere, Mom."

She was chopping my name off, a warning that something about our relationship was problematic at this precise moment.

So I shrugged out of my backpack, planted my bottom on the ground between the soles of my boots, leaned back against the pack, and opened my canteen to take a lengthy, well-deserved swig of water. Something should have warned me, something about the way my daughter looked long and hard in my direction then swept up her pack and replanted her feet on the path as I stretched first one leg, then the other, out in front of me and poured Sam's water onto a piece of plastic set down in a small bowl-shaped hole beside my hip. Something should have looked ominous about the way she set her chin and glared at those treetops and seemed to have forgotten her thirst intact, something, anything. But nothing did. So I was still half lying there, guzzling water and soaking up the warmth of the late summer sun, when Ruth peeled off down the trail hollering out, "Last one to the oasis is a rotten egg!" and Sam took out after her so fast he kicked gravel all over his makeshift bowl and my legs.

Scrambling to my feet, I yelled after them, "Don't let him get in the water!"

Ruth stopped so abruptly Sam ran directly into the backs of her knees.

"I know the rules, Mom. I'm not a dunderhead," she shouted, looking intensely at me and putting one hand on one hip.

Then, turning on her heel, she fastened the other hand in Sam's collar and called out over her shoulder, "You're still the rotten egg."

In our family, being the rotten egg relegates you to worker-bee status. Ruth had just covered the last two hundred yards of our first four miles faster than I could swallow and stand up. She was now officially Queen of this trip.

Any mother who has unwillingly lost a child lives always beneath the shadow of that terror. Even when the child comes home, fear seeps into your every gesture: You hug her a little too tightly, hold on a little too long, laugh a little too hard at all her jokes, let slide her small moments of defiance, and get way too unnerved when she slips out of sight unexpectedly. Sensory overload. Small wonder that your parental antennae miss the more subtle cues, ones that hint you're being challenged to a race you're about to lose, for instance. Rotten egg—it wasn't simply a metaphor for my rank until sundown. Ruth was finally home and I was catching up. In more ways than one.

When I finally dragged myself into the oasis, Ruth and Sam were perched side by side on a rock, calmly sharing a box of raisins. They paused only long enough for the Daughter Queen to chide and point, "Rotten Egg." Then, same finger trained on herself, she added, "Major Queen."

I curtsied, dropped my pack again, and grumbled something about her having gained the throne through questionable means. Ruth merely raised her right eyebrow dismissively, but as soon as I looked away, she giggled behind her hand. Then she slid down off her quartz monzonite throne, her shepherd-mix gentleman in waiting loping after her, and for the next two hours we all puttered about the oasis.

There's something primeval and lonesome about finding a small pool of murky, insect-strewn water nestled reluctantly at the bottom of a desert canyon that the word "oasis" can never articulate. Although only the most powerful of thirsts could make this liquid appear potable, its presence alone gives the setting a touch of serene authenticity, a feel of deeply rooted connections to those dark, cool streams that flow beneath the parched skin of the ground on which you stand wondering at water's generosity, marveling that it agrees to come to the surface at all, much less stays long enough to collect dead twigs and bugs and algae. Tall swishing grasses grow near the pool's edge, slicing at your legs, and the heavy brush skirts of the fan palms rustle and sway in the contrary breezes that come dueling down the wash, tumbling over themselves and anything else that stands alongside you and the rocks and trees.

I always feel like I'm in church, perched on the very first pew, when I stand at the edge of an oasis. Here God is generous, worth kneeling for and knowing, and is as deeply saddened by cruelty and thoughtlessness as any of the rest of us are—and I know this with a ferocity that surprises even my most determinedly agnostic self. On that day, I ventured to voice some of those thoughts aloud and said, "Sometimes I think I can almost feel God here."

Ruth spun around on one toe and glared at me. I waited. Finally my daughter's response came, sheathed in a frown that went from the top of her head to the soles of her feet, "Hmpfh. I'm just about sick of God."

There was no need to ask why, no chance to either.

Ruth rushed onward, "Been praying to him a long, long time, and he just about doesn't never do what I ask. Lets Daddy hurt us and stuff. Lets the judge and the cops act ugly to us too. So I think God's a meany, and one day I'm gonna meet him and tell him so, face front."

Face front. Ruth has been heading into life that way from the moment she landed on the planet and urinated on my half-blind, nearly retired obstetrician. There's not a dissembling cell in my daughter's whole body, a trait I've always admired in her, but one I also knew had cost her many harsh punishments over the last two years.

Slowly nodding, I said, "I guess I can see why you'd think that. But, you know, God isn't just a man. God's a woman too, and everything else that we can't even dream up in our heads. It's mostly people that have made God into a man, rewritten books and histories so everyone would forget that God is both female and male."

Ruth tipped her head to one side, considering this, and leaned over to scratch Sam's head.

"Nope, he has to be a man, Mom. He's too mean to be a woman."

Then, chin set at a stubborn angle, she turned on her heel, Sam in tow, and headed off to look at a small kangaroo rat's nest they'd found nearby.

Breathing in strongly of the heated air, I settled down not far from the sweeping base of a palm tree and lay back on the ground to gaze at the sky, wondering aloud what new tasks my daughter would come up with for her Rotten Egg. Except for a sharp glance or two Ruth ignored me clean, pulled her tiny notebook out of her shirt pocket, and said, "Time for me to get back to work. The botany's waiting."

My response was automatic.

"You mean the plants or the subject?"

"The plants."

"That's flora then. If you're talking about the plants—botany's the name of the subject, flora's the word for plants in general. Flora or vegetation maybe."

Ruth's tone dropped immediately to the register for explaining a basic fact to a simpleton.

"I know that, Mom. Read those words in my book, but don't like 'em very much. I like botany better."

This was too good an opportunity to pass up.

"What's wrong with flora?"

Ruth wrinkled up her nose and paused a moment, then said, "Yeulckk—it sounds like cottage cheese, and that stuff's nasty."

"Oh. But what about vegetation?"

For this one, Ruth had to think awhile. Hand looped through one pack strap, she gazed off into the sky and finally said, "Well, that sounds like vegetables too much, and they're all nasty too. All but spinach."

Ruth was into spinach, had requested it two meals a day ever since the first night she'd arrived home. Frank, the park ranger I'd married a few months earlier, had told her that spinach is what made Popeye so strong.

She continued, "So botany's better," and, without waiting for me to reply, she spun around on her heel and took off again.

"Botany it is then," I called after her, laughing and wishing once more that kids had the wheel of the lexicon. Ever since I was six myself and learned in first grade that adults had full control of the language I've been resisting that unjust arrangement.

A few yards away, Ruth stopped short, did a little hop step, looked back over her shoulder, and brought me back to the present again with a skip and a question.

"So what do you think about the name Felicity, Mom?"

I groaned aloud, Ruth laughed and skipped off with Sam close behind.

This name change business was beginning to sound serious, so I knew I'd have to address it head-on before too long. The very first thing Ruth had announced to Frank and me on her arrival was that she had decided to change her name, "So I'll be trying on some new ones for a while till I can find the one I want best," she said.

When asked why, she answered unhesitatingly, "I want a strong name, a name so nobody will think I'm a wimp and they can beat up on me and stuff."

Hot, flashing streams of pain coursing through me, I flinched visibly, turning partially away so Ruth wouldn't see it, but she was looking at Sam and wouldn't have noticed anyway. She kept right on talking.

"It's like you, Mommy. You have a soft name, and you're nice to everybody, kind of sissy, so people beat up on you. I want a hard name so nobody even tries anymore," she'd said, voice toughening as she looked me in the eye and stopped stroking Sam's fur to finish the thought. "And I'm gonna get big and strong and mean as a snake so I can whup on 'em if they do." Almost as an afterthought, she added, "And I'll protect you and Jon too."

I had no words then, no words except another murmured apology for the past two years of her life, and a hug to tell her how dreadfully I'd missed her. Tears standing in her eyes, Ruth locked her arms around my neck almost fiercely and said, "I missed you too, Mommy."

Frank acted instinctively and gave both my daughter and me precisely what we both needed right then. A huge bear hug. Then he took a long stride backward and broke into a wide grin. "Well," he said, "why don't I start teaching you some of the ways that cops like me use to deal with the bad guys?"

Ruth yelped out a cheer so loud that Sam leapt to his feet, while I grinned but excused myself to the bathroom where I could throw up. By the time I'd washed my face and returned to the front room, Ruth was executing her first "takedown" of a grown man and she was beaming. If she is determined to change her name, I decided, so be it.

Still, I'd almost changed my mind since, especially when we rolled through some of her considerations, some of which I was quite sure she'd chosen just to horrify me: Tiffany, Bast, Athena,

Deborah, Hera, Alex, Calypso, Frogger, Sam, and now Felicity, Most of these Ruth used only for a few hours, then moved on to another choice. Most were strong women's names, "Grumpy goddesses," Ruth opined, "just like me."

Now, on our weekend alone together, Felicity had come out of the blue, or rather, out of the tiny baby name book that Ruth had worn to a bedraggled mess from paging through it so much. Time for me to speak up. Tonight, I vowed, tonight I'll start telling her Mammaw Ruth's stories again. Then I rolled over on my side and soaked up more of the heated air, confident that Sam was looking out for his new missus.

The loss of anyone we love hurts, but nothing bears any comparison to losing a child. When Ruth and Jon disappeared, I felt as if all that was human about my spirit had been laid open and flayed. The flaying rips open your protective layers, sears your nerve endings, makes your innermost organs shriek mutely. Once flayed, the skin of your soul grows back hesitantly, if at all, and even in the unlikely, miraculous off-chance that the child is returned, as one of mine was, your spirit remains ever-sensitive to touch, instinctively shying away from memories of the event much as a badly burned finger recoils from an open flame. Once flayed, you must teach yourself to trust beyond the loss with every breath that comes.

Loss is not a foreign concept among my people, the hardworking, rural Southerners who brought me into the world and nurtured me through my first seventeen years. Wakes and funerals were as common in our county as Sunday dinner on the ground and Saturday night's Grand Ole Opry on the radio, but not near so much fun or with half as much to recommend them. My sister and I had to wear long dark-colored dresses and socks to these death events even in the summertime, and tight patent-leather shoes, in which we were expected to stand around for what seemed like (and actually were) hours on end. Funerals were things you just did to show respect if you were a Southerner of good breeding, so we both grumbled but we did them anyhow and got good at it.

Then, a few years later, death claimed the woman I loved more than anyone on the planet, besides my father, my horse, and my raccoon, that is—my mother's mother, Mammaw Ruth to me. She was part American Indian and part something else that she point-blank refused to acknowledge or name. On the dreary December morning that she closed her eyes and never opened them again, I finally understood why we had to wear dark clothing to funerals: all other colors tell lies at a time when you really need to be bumping noses with the truth.

Mammaw's death punched a hole in my world, introduced me up close to the whole prolonged business of dying from cancer, broke my heart, nudged me to live better, and gave me my best reason to date for trying to land in heaven when I was done with living. She'd gone ahead of me, that was all, I reasoned, long after we had covered her plain coffin with damp black dirt in the cold drizzle from a sky I was absolutely certain would never again welcome back the sun. I truly believed the world had stopped right along with Mammaw's heart, and I numbly plodded through the day of her funeral feeling very little, noticing nothing at all but those cascading red roses that I despised with every cell of my body. It took years to make sense of her "passing," years to make peace with the loss, years to believe that she was gone from sight and touch, from smell and hearing, but otherwise not gone at all.

To this day, I yearn for the feel of her strong, gnarled hand on my shoulder or head, the sound of her deep, rasping voice telling me her Indian stories, the sight of her big old belly jiggling with laughter underneath her flour-spattered apron. But I remain unflayed. It's the child for which you've cared and loved and lived and breathed that lays you open to that. So I lay on the desert floor, one child home and doing botany, one still gone, and carried myself back over the decades to where my head was cradled in Mammaw's lap while she shelled butter beans in a big tin dishpan just above my face and told me story after story of how her people came to be in this world.

Ear pressed to the ground for no better reason than that I'm always curious to see how close someone has to be before I can feel them approaching, I listened to my daughter come marching toward me. She was scuffing her feet, which meant she was getting sleepy too. Sure enough, in a couple minutes, she plopped down on the ground beside me, and Sam stretched out between us. Now our trip was fully under way.

Deserts demand siestas. Even a live wire like Ruthie can't evade the convincing urge for a nap that reaches out invisibly and gives you a warm hug whenever the sun starts its long slide toward the western horizon. Ruth, Sam, and I were curled up near the shady edge of a big boulder, sleeping intermittently, watching the palm fronds lift and wave slightly in the wind.

Something inarticulate occurs when you rest outside in a desert. All that's petty drops away from you, like a dry old skin sheds off a rattler, leaving her shiny and young again, if momentarily sightless and off balance. You blink the sleep out of your eyes to see with an unexpected clarity and suck in great tingling gulps of newly unearthed oxygen. I always stretch—long, gradual, semi-deliberate lengthenings of each muscle group—and feel keenly the sand grains biting into my back or arm or leg. It's a powerful way of coming to terms with the parts of my existence that defy explanation, this ability to lie steady, noiselessly, on a tiny bit of ground in a land that many people shun and fear as too harsh, too forbidding to even walk in or visit, much less sit down or sleep on. Sometimes, if I'm still enough, spiders use me as an anchoring point for a new web addition: that's what was happening that day. Grateful the Queen wasn't awake to squawk the poor creature into retreat, I lay on my side and watched the small fearless fellow throw himself off the limb of his creosote bush home and touch down lightly on my thigh. Now a thin gossamer strand connected me to the bush, and as I watched, the spider headed back up the filigreed cable.

All of a sudden, Ruth screamed and sat straight up, and I sat up right along with her. Lord only knows where the hapless spider landed.

"What is it?" I asked, alarmed when it became apparent Ruth wasn't protesting the spider's presence—as near as I could tell, she appeared not even to have seen him.

She kept screaming, flailing with her hands, hitting me, Sam, herself even. Grabbing her arms, I shook her sharply, and as quickly as she'd started the outburst, Ruth stopped, her body went limp beneath my hands, and she looked into my eyes and finally saw me.

I waited. Slowly, with difficulty, she opened her mouth and whispered, with tears shimmering in her eyes and pouring down her cheeks, "He's hurting Jon again."

Instinctively, I sucked air into my lungs and looked into the abyss of my daughter's eyes, seeing there a pain that mirrored my own. I knew then that she, too, had felt this lash, that the screaming agony of losing a child is not, indeed, the worst thing that can happen to a person: Ruth had lost her brother, and she grieved for him every bit as deeply as I, his mother, ever could. We sat in shuddering silence. Sam stepped from one of us to the other, settling his head first on Ruth's shoulder, then on mine, and finally he lay down so his body would be touching both of us simultaneously.

I had no heart to lie, to tell my daughter the kind of senseless soothing words both she and I knew were false anyway. There was a very good chance Ruth was right, that even as we snoozed and reconnected in the desert, her brother was being beaten for some tiny, real or imagined infraction of his father's rules. Maybe he hadn't folded his T-shirts neatly enough this morning. Or had left a spot on one of the glasses. Or had been beat up by a bully at school.

For long, untimed moments, we sat hunched in the sand, silent and sober, both lost in our own worlds of longing and sadness. After a while I took Ruth's hand in mine and said what I always did: "One day Jon will come home to us, Ruthie. One day he will."

Ruth listened gravely, then looked up at me and replied, "Yeah." After a long while she added, "And then he'll be a thorn back in my neck again, huh Mommy? Always bossing me around, stuff like that."

"Undoubtedly," I said, smiling at her, grateful that of all the maternal traits she could have wound up with, Ruth had somehow gotten the best one, an unflinching pragmatism.

Ruth responded by squeezing my hands and then scrambling to her feet.

"He's a knucklehead, but I guess he can't help it. He is just a boy," she said, as if that explained everything. She stalked off. "Now I need to get back to the botany."

I rolled over and listened to her footsteps retreating, and closed my eyes against the tears that kept rushing in, and listened hard for my son. Before long, I was dozing again.

Minutes later I stretched awkwardly and opened my eyes, feeling heartsore and stiff, but refreshed and ready to get up—and looked directly into Ruth's and Sam's faces. Ruth broke eye contact only long enough to check her watch, and I could tell from her expression that that wasn't the first time she'd done that lately.

"You've slept twelve whole minutes, Mom!" she grouched. "Don't you think it's time we found us a place to camp tonight?"

Next thing I knew we'd shrugged back into our packs and were heading down toward Victory Palms. We scrambled up the canyon's southwest side so we could find a good campsite, far enough away from the oasis that our presence wouldn't frighten any animals who depended on it. Ruth was hiking now like a seasoned pro. No longer on a trail she knew, no longer in a hurry, she even slowed down and stopped periodically to look behind her so she'd have some idea where we'd come from if we got lost. I'd taught her that again the very day she came home.

"So you track people, Mommy. Do you ever get lost?" she asked, referring to the fact that I had taken up search-and-rescue tracking for the National Park Service in her absence.

"Well, I'm sort of paid not to," I replied.

"But do you?" Ruth asked again and stopped walking entirely, waiting for my answer. It didn't take a functioning genius to know she would be deciding whether or not to continue following me based on what my answer was.

Luckily, I could reassure her with the truth and say, "No," because Ruth can spot a lie at thirty paces, and there were only twelve between us.

"Well, good," she said, and I heard her feet start hitting the ground behind me again.

We soon found a spacious level area with plenty of small boulders scattered thoughtfully about its edges for camp furniture. By the time I'd fired up our tiny Primus stove, Ruth had set our "table," with Sam sitting patiently beside her. Long before the sun was anywhere near gone, we had finished supper and were playing hopscotch. I lost, but that was only because the Queen chose to exercise her right to order me to put both feet down on the ground NOW! just as I was closing in on a well-deserved win. Sam received his first-place trophy from the royal highness herself, then came over to console me as I grumbled some more about monarchical privilege.

"What about the name Bast?" Ruth asked suddenly, referring to an Egyptian cat goddess she'd recently met in a library book. Striking a goddess pose that was remarkable only for the height at which she managed to hold her nose in the air, Ruth said imperiously, "I am Bast, goddess of all I see. And some that I can't."

So we were back to Bast. It was time for me to speak up, so finally I said what I'd been thinking all week.

"But tell me true now, why do you want to change your name? I think it's one of the prettiest names I ever heard—one of the strongest, too. I wish it were mine even."

"Good then. You can have it."

"I'm not going to take my own daughter's name, mizzle head. You didn't answer my question. Ruth's a strong name—why do you want to change it?"

"Don't like it."

"Why not?"

"It's not pretty, it's plain. Just Ruth. I want a pretty name, a song name maybe," she said and burst into a tuneless "Help me Rhonda, help help me, Rhonda." "Maybe Rhonda would work. Now you see? Isn't that better than Ruth, just Ruth?"

Before I even had a chance to answer, she hurried on, "I want a big name, too. Not a weak name like yours, Mommy. People are mean to you, and you just let 'em be. But I'm gonna be different. Strong. Punch 'em in the nose maybe."

For the second time in ten days I saw myself through my daughter's eyes. She really meant it. She had a weakling for a mom. A wimp. No matter that I avoid most confrontations largely because I feel they're a waste of spirit and spit. No matter, either, that my reasons for refusing to fight back against her father on my own behalf were based on my strict adherence to principles of nonviolence. My way had worked reasonably well, too, during the six years of our marriage anyway, because he beat only me, not the children. But Ruth saw the inside of her world, had to reckon with the blunt fact of living with her father without me there to absorb his anger, and from that angle, in her eyes and my own as well, I must surely come up wanting.

No matter that I had done my dead-level best to find Jon and Ruth and bring them home, but wound up out of money, very ill, and hopelessly outmaneuvered by a justice system that would rather have children beaten regularly than intervene between a biological father and his offspring. No matter any of the reasons or justifications. Ruth sincerely believed she had a wimp for a mom. Gritting my teeth to hold back the vomit, I told myself sternly that this attitude would serve her well in the long run: if she kept up this tack, held onto these insights, no man would ever beat her again. Meantime, I had a job to do, and it was close enough to bedtime to begin it.

"Ruthie, I feel like there's a long, wide canyon running between us, a canyon like Lost Palms, only bigger and deeper, and it doesn't have a name. It's like we were holding hands and walking along together until the day your father kidnapped you two years ago, and then all of a sudden you were over there on one side and I was over here. Do you know what I mean?"

Ruth nodded, then looked directly at me and said, "He told us you didn't love us no more."

"What did you think about that?"

"I hollered at him that it was a lie, but he beated me bad for it, Mommy, hitted me with the broom."

"I can't fix that hurt, Ruth. I can't even give the canyon between us a name, but I can tell you that you were telling the truth. I have always loved you and your brother, from before either one of you was ever born, loved you more than anything else in the world. Nothing has ever changed that; nothing ever will. Do you believe me?"

She nodded slightly. We'd already had a couple versions of this conversation by then, so Ruth had a fair idea of how hard I'd tried to bring her and her brother home again.

"So I am very sorry that I seem weak to you now, but someday I hope you'll see that I have pretty good reasons for being the way I am. Doesn't make it perfect, but it works for me, and we'll sit down and talk about all that when you're ready. But now we need to get back to this name change thing. Do you remember all the stories I told you when you were little?" I asked.

"Umhm," Ruth nodded, smiling widely.

She did remember very well. She'd asked for one backrub and four stories a night every night since she'd been home, so I knew she remembered them.

"Remember I told you once those were my grandmother's stories?"

"Yes."

"Well, I think it's time you learned a little more about her." Ruth shuffled her bottom around and trained her shining eyes on me.

"Mammaw's name was Ruth Haney. She was an Indian, born in Mississippi in 1899 and lived there all her life, so you can guess she had to be one of the toughest, meanest women on the planet just to survive—"

"Daddy said she was just a stupid old sharecropper without no schooling," Ruth interjected. "And he said you sound stupid when you call her Mammaw, too. Says that's a name only uneducated people use."

"Well, I think words like 'Mammaw' are proud and important, and you need to use them as often as you can, because English needs all the help it can get. It gets downright sick in the head if some of us don't break its rules regularly, know what I mean?"

"Yes ma'am," Ruth said. She'd heard my views on the language before.

"That means you say 'ain't' and 'Mammaw' and 'Lawsy Mercy!' and whatever else you can think of that sounds like the normal people around you, and you just flat-out ignore your schoolteachers when they tell you any different. If you get in trouble, I'll back you up on it, all right?"

"All-righty, I b'lieve I got it, lawsy mercy I do!" Ruth was now so happy she was pounding her fists with excitement on the ground, ready to jump into the conversation with both feet.

"Good."

"I'm Indian too, Mommy—got a card that says so."

"Yep, you're a registered Potowatomi—that's a little bit different from Mammaw Ruth, and she didn't ever get a card, but that's just one more thing you two have in common. Now what you really need to know is that four months before you were born, I knew you would be a girl—don't know how I knew it, I just did. Knew deep inside that you'd be an ornery, knotheaded little girl just like I was when I was your age, exactly like Mammaw Ruth was all her life. And I made up my mind right then that you would be named after her." Pausing a moment to let that sink in, I went on, "Now, I'm not about to sit here and tell you you can't change your name. You can, if that's what you really want to do and you ever find one that you'll stick with for more than three hours." Ruth grinned and tossed her head around defiantly. I was right. She had been gigging me with some of those choices.

I continued, "But if you do decide to change it, I want you to do it knowing full well that the name you're choosing to set aside is the finest, most special name of the finest, most special woman who ever set a foot on this planet. Ruth Haney. And it just so happens that she was the strongest person I've ever known, too. Tough as nails, with a backbone of steel and a heart to match, she used to say. Didn't let anybody walk on her or hers either. So if you throw away her name, you'll be throwing away all that strength, and you'll have to get some more on your own. So you need to think about this name change really hard before you go on with it, okay?"

Finally I sat quiet, spent from my outburst. Ruth nodded, crawled over and sat beside me, and said, "Mommy, I really think it's about bedtime, don't you?"

"Sure," I said, looking up at the four o'clock sun shining down on our heads. "Sounds fine by me."

Whooping and hollering, Ruth rushed over to her cotton mat and waited almost patiently for me to sit down and pull off my shoes, then lie back on my own mat beside her. Sam looked at us as if we were crazy, and he stood there at our feet for a couple minutes, but when we didn't get up, he finally stretched out between us, chin on his paws but still ready in case we came to our senses and got up to finish out the day.

"Storytime!" Ruth chortled, and I groaned and rolled over on my back, pretending to be really sleepy.

"Come on, Mommy—tell me a story, one of Mammaw Ruth's stories."

I groaned again, and Ruth upped the ante. "I'll let you off being the Rotten Egg."

"As well you should, too. You cheated anyhow," I said, covering my eyes so I wouldn't glimpse my daughter's face and inadvertently laugh.

"Okay, then tell me six stories in a row, and I'll promise not to cheat you anymore. Anymore this week."

I lost the round exactly as I'd planned to. Within minutes we were deeply immersed in Mammaw Ruth's stories. By the time the moon stood full over us, my throat was so hoarse I could hardly talk, and Ruth finally fell fast asleep in the crook of my arm. These are the hours that help you forget the flaying, help you remember the hope. Desert nights don't simply promise healing; they practice it. They give you a chance to sink inside the regenerative contours of the earth itself, to step outside the demanding rush of society, conversation, automobiles, human noise, and smells, and your own expectations of yourself, and simply breathe yourself back from the brink.

The next morning, I woke with the sun and made a cup of tea. An hour later I poked my sleepy daughter and said, "Well, get up, lazy head, the day's half gone."

Ruth groaned, and I reminded her that she'd wanted us to find a boulder to practice climbing on today.

Ignoring that entirely, she sat up, hair tousled, eyes still half shut, and said, "I dreamed about Jon last night, Mommy."

"You did?" I said, voice determinedly flat.

"He was here too, right here with us, listening to Mammaw's stories. We were sitting right there on the ground telling them, and you know what happened?!" Ruth's eyes were now wide as saucers, not a trace of sleepiness left in them. I didn't even have time to shake my head in response to her question before she burst onward.

"Mammaw Ruth come walking up, from right over down by Victory Palms! She walked right on up here big as day, wearing that big white apron and walking beside her big old white bulldog, and you know what she did? She sat herself right by me and said to that dog, 'Now Baby Boy, you behave yourself and don't beat up on their scrawny little yellow city mutt'—that's what she said about Samson," Ruth gulped and paused for air, but rushed on again. "And then she hiked her dress up over one knee and said, 'I hear yall been tellin my stories over here,' and we said, 'Yes'm' real quiet, just like so. She nodded her head again and said, 'Well, yall got some of the p'ticulars wrong, and I'm here to set you younguns straight.' That's what she said, Mommy!" Ruth was talking so fast she could hardly sit still. Finally she gave up trying, scrambled to her feet, and rushed over to where I was sitting.

"Sure sounds like Mammaw Ruth to me," I replied. "What else did she say?"

"Oh, well, she just told us every single one of her stories again and fixed the p'ticulars you missed—you didn't miss anything important though, don't worry."

Ruth was starting to settle down slightly, so I offered her some granola for breakfast, which she gobbled down so quickly I thought she might be sick, suggested as much, and was rewarded with a grin but nothing else in the way of compliance. Then I broached the topic of rock climbing again, and Ruth thought a long while about it. Thought so long I had our bed mats and sheeting rolled and stowed away in my pack before she answered.

"It's like this, Mommy," she finally said, "there's rocks we can climb near home."

"Yes. So what are you saying?"

"I want to go home. Maybe we'll get a message from Jon."

"But this was supposed to be a weekend camping trip," I protested. "Three days to spend just us together in the desert, figuring out a way to cross that no-name canyon between us and such."

"Well, we can do that at home easy as here, can't we?" Ruth asked, so reasonably I couldn't argue.

"Sure we can, I guess," I said. She was right, after all. One patch of desert isn't necessarily any more special than the next. Given that we lived in Park Service housing, with only a radio for communication, it took a while for phone messages to get to us anyhow. And even longer for us to drive to a phone where we could respond. If Jon was trying to reach us, we'd never know it way out here. For the first time ever, I regretted living inside a national park. Ruth knew full well what I was thinking. She followed it up with a sensible suggestion.

"Well then, let's go home."

"Home it is," I agreed. We hoisted our packs and headed back for the canyon. Reaching it, Ruth took the lead and kept us all moving at a fast clip for about four miles straight. When we passed Mastodon Peak, a small chunky rock hill near Cottonwood Springs, about half a mile from home, Ruth finally stopped and said, "Whew! I'm really thirsty!"

"Too thirsty to walk and drink at the same time anymore?" I asked skeptically, since that's what she'd had us doing the whole way.

"Yep."

"I don't know. Sounds like a trap to me. Hey Sam!" I called. "What do you think? Is she angling to be Queen again here or what?"

Ruth giggled and spilled water down her shirt, and Sam wagged his tail happily, ready to go or stay. He didn't appear to care much which right then.

"Come sit over here by me, Mommy," Ruth said. "It's not a trick, promise, needle in the eye and stuff."

I warily set my pack down and eased over to her, while Ruth basked in the glory of yesterday's successful subterfuge. But she didn't move.

When I got properly seated beside her, she reached over and took my hand and said, "That no-name canyon? The one you talked about?"

I nodded and she went on.

"I was thinking we should give it a name."

"Oh," I said, caught entirely off guard. Ruth held onto my hand firmly with one of hers, and patted it absentmindedly with the other.

"I was thinking we could call it Knucklehead Palms, Mommy. What do you think?"

I said the first thing that came to mind. "But it doesn't have any palms in it."

Ruth looked taken aback momentarily, but she recovered quickly and said, "It does now. Mammaw Ruth planted a couple last night when she come by."

"Oh. Okay then, I like that name, I guess. Fits pretty well."

But Ruth wasn't finished.

"And Mommy, I was thinking maybe it'd be better if I don't change my name for now. I can wait till I get older, I think."

"All right," I said. Then warily I added, "How old?"

"Oh, maybe when I'm ten or so. Ten's real old, huh?"

I was just about to agree with her, to say ten was practically ancient, in the range of Methuselah at least, just about to let her know I was glad she'd decided to wait and how proud I was of her and how happy I was she was home, just verging on saying that whole set of lovely, mushy things . . . when Ruth leapt to her feet, snatched up her pack, and yelled back over her shoulder, "Last one to Cottonwood Springs is a Rotten Egg!"

Her ponytail and Sam's tail rounded the first bend simultaneously ten seconds later, about the time I made it to my feet, and I could hear Ruth laughing proudly, the sound staccato-like and retreating as her feet pounded the ground.

Clearly I still had some catching up to do. I shouldered my pack and galloped off down the path toward home, heading up the far side of Knucklehead Canyon at last.

Identity

Going Solo

by Wendy Knight

I stare at the oversized atlas at the travel clinic, waiting for my body to safely absorb the inoculations I've received, my eyes searching for Kenya and Sudan, where in a few short weeks I will be researching a story on Sudan's civil war. I'll be visiting refugee camps and field sites, so the required list of vaccinations is long and I return to the clinic frequently. Each visit, I study the topography and political borders intently, tracing previous journeys—the Wind River Range, Menorca; making new discoveries—the Ural Mountains, the Sargasso Sea, the Cook Islands; and meditating on the longer list of adventures I crave—paddling the South China Sea, climbing the Alaska Range, sailing the Turquoise Coast, walking the Kalahari Desert. The sand-colored mountains and blue-veined rivers stay with me long after I leave.

With no adverse reactions to the shots, I race to pick up my thirteen-year-old daughter from school. Alex and I share an active life—soccer matches, orthodontist appointments, and similar patterns of motherhood fill my usual weeks. I find it incredibly rewarding, being a mom, one of those experiences you can never fully grasp until you breathe it yourself, and I am routinely struck by the profound meaning I derive from it, in its ying-yang of simplicity and enormity. Seemingly banal tasks, like packing her lunch in the morning or driving her to school, bring me an unqualified joy. But my frequent trips leave her dubious, I think, about my maternal commitment, despite the lunches and soccer games.

A couple of years ago, Alex and I were lounging on a beach-side hammock at the Mauna Lani Bay Hotel on the Big Island, the Pacific fluttering onto shore in the fading day, in one of those quiet moments when truth is revealed.

"I don't like when you go away," she announced, referring to my frequent work trips.

I generally plan these when she's with her dad, with whom I share joint custody.

"You're with your dad anyway," I reasoned.

"Not always."

She wasn't conceding. We swayed quietly for a moment.

"Why don't you like when I travel?" I probed.

She grew still and shifted her gaze to the sand below.

"I'm afraid you won't come back," she confessed, tears spilling down her pale skin.

I was stunned. She sensed it, more profoundly than others—my perpetual urge to flee. Not from her necessarily but from the parameters, expectations, demands, and definitions that confine me to a conventional life.

When I was twenty-six, fully ensconced in a rewarding health-policy job in Washington, D.C., married to a wonderful man, a sweet toddler asleep in her crib, I read an obituary of an elderly women—Josephine, I think, was her name—in the *New York Times.* As a young teenager, she had learned to fly, eventually becoming an airmail pilot. When she was seventeen, she hijacked her father's plane and flew to Africa. She hunted big game in Africa and Asia, once shooting and killing a tiger that charged her sister. It went on like this for two columns. A sickening hunger grew from within. I wanted a life like that.

The phone rings. My daughter's tearful voice is on the other end.

"I don't like being at my dad's on Fridays," she wails uncharacteristically. Perhaps it's teenage hormones, a rough day at school, or the anxiety of my impending departure.

"No one's here. My dad doesn't get here till six," comes this unspoken, tearful plea for my company from a child who routinely denies the existence of emotions, hers and mine.

In the throes of finishing a book manuscript, deprived of sleep, computer guy here to fix the worthless computer, toilet clogged, kitchen a wreck, I leave it all and drive to her dad's house ten minutes up the road to retrieve her. Richard's car is there when I arrive; he's just arrived, too. As I walk into the house, Richard and

I pass each other knowing looks, as connected parents often do. Alex sits at the kitchen table, teary.

"I tried to call you," she offers apologetically, knowing of my recent heavy workload.

"It's okay," I tell her warmly and move towards her, caressing her head gently.

"Anytime," I say, kissing her cheek.

I want her to know I'll always be there for her. So I repeat the words.

"Anytime you need me, you call me." I squeeze her tightly.

She nods in relief, tears returning to their hidden well.

When children reach adolescence, parents brace for the anticipated snotty remarks, eye-rolling, and general abhorrence of our existence. But Alex usually still wants me around, for which I am very grateful. I watch other kids retreat to their rooms after dinner, escaping parental presence like I often did, but she stays in the kitchen chattering about school and such as I clean up.

"Let's play a game," she suggests, honoring our post-dinner winter tradition. Come November, we play cards or Scrabble or Yahtzee for an hour before she reads and I work some more. All the while, we joke and laugh and talk easily, sometimes seriously about her homework or an issue with a friend, other times about the silly antics of eighth-grade boys. Then she goes upstairs and prepares for bed.

"Mom, I'm ready."

It's the same call each time. I climb the steep farmhouse steps to her bedroom.

"Good night, sweetie," I say, pulling the blankets around her shoulders.

I lean down to kiss her. She tilts her head towards me and we meet halfway with a smooch.

"I love you."

"I love you, too."

"See you in the morning."

Another night. Another ritual.

It is moments like these I cherish most.

Two weeks before Christmas. The African trip is fast approaching. Crushed with work, I ponder aloud not attending the holiday concert we've been planning, thinking I usually drag her to these things anyway.

"Nooo," she protests. "You're canceling everything—working out, my doctor's appointment, the concert . . . " she goes on.

I see how important our time is to her, how the upcoming trip and my work have her feeling neglected.

"You're right," I concede, "we'll go."

As I drive into town, she asks me about Africa, something she has yet to do.

"What are you doing there?" she wants to know.

I tell her I'm going to work on some stories about the war.

"I know that," she continues, "but what are you going to do while you're there?"

She wants specifics. I explain that I'll be with a relief organization in Sudan talking with humanitarian aid workers, observing them while they dole out food and medicines to villagers at various field sites in South Sudan, meeting Sudanese families who've been devastated by the civil war. Feverishly, I tell her about the conflict in Sudan, how millions of people have been displaced, villages raided, children kidnapped and enslaved, bombs dropped. She looks at me with concern and in an instant I realize I've gone too far, impassioned by the opportunity to tell these stories to her, to the world.

"But not anymore, right?" she inquires. "Not now?"

No, I tell her, not now. I'll be fine, I assure her. There's a cease-fire. Peace talks in Kenya. I wonder how much of this registers, if she's only heard that I'm traveling to a country where people are kidnapped, starved, killed.

So determined am I to live a conscious life, I forget that I must refute reality at times, if not for me then for my child. This winter, I read an online news flash about an ice-climbing death.

"Shit," I muttered, unthinkingly, aloud.

"What?" she wanted to know. Foolishly, I told her. She shot me a look; "that's what you do," her eyes said. How can I explain my desire to climb frozen waterfalls, travel to war-torn countries, paddle the broad lake at night, pursue things that take me away from her? For a day, week, month, maybe someday permanently. Prematurely.

2:00 A.M. I'm nestled between flannel sheets, admiring the moon's iridescent blue-silver sheen on my bedroom walls. I have long imagined a visit to Africa, the first glimpse of a lion or elephant beyond a *National Geographic* video, retiring to a tented camp, cold beer in hand, after a day of game-watching.

But this virgin journey to the Dark Continent will take me to its underbelly—refugee camps in Kenya and health clinics in Sudan, a country ravaged by a twenty-year civil war. After four months of planning, I finally allow thoughts of angry men wielding AK-47s and government warplanes dropping bombs to ease into my tired, cluttered mind.

"Safety is an illusion," I am fond of saying these days.

It's a form of denial, a lame attempt to reject my conscious role in living adventurously.

"You're crazy," the computer guy laughed when I mentioned my plans for Africa earlier that day.

I am crazy. Crazy to have willingly assumed the absurdly awesome responsibility of nurturing another life, of so completely and purely loving someone whose absence from my life would be unbearable. Crazy to travel halfway around the globe to witness the unfathomable consequences of inhumanity, and to insert myself in its wretched path.

* * *

My father died of lung cancer in May 2000 after a six-month struggle that coincided with the end of my relationship with a man I deeply loved. The events of the preceding months had left me utterly exhausted and heartbroken, so I planned to spend two weeks hiking and camping alone in the West, to contemplate my unraveled life.

Understandably, my family and friends were apprehensive about my venturing in the wilderness solo.

"Camping? Alone?" "Are you sure this is a good idea?" "Maybe you should carry a gun." "What if you sprain your ankle?"

The first night of the trip, a Great Plains sky unleashed a violent thunderstorm, filling my tent with rain so heavy and insistent it seemed to pour in from my own grieved soul. The next day, I kayaked the lazy Niobrara River in the sand hills of Nebraska, a family of otters, some mule deer, and a blue heron my only companions on the twenty-mile stretch. Desert sagebrush aromas wafted into my campsite each night in the Badlands, and I lay in the darkness intoxicated from the earthy perfume, listening to the lonely yips of nearby coyotes.

Traveling without companions sharpened my awareness of the landscape—a stranger's look, the vast night sky, a twitching branch, the smell of a dense pine forest freshly dampened with rain. Alone for days on end, stripped of the roles I traditionally inhabit—mother, sister, daughter, ex-wife—I was whole in my familial nakedness. In this remote and barren land, I was inspired by a serenity I have rarely achieved, consumed by an irresistible taste of wanderlust that tears at me still.

A lovable, captivating daughter wrenches me the other way, and 9/11 only intensified Alex's dislike of my travels. It was two months before I boarded another plane against her fervent protests. Since that dreadful day, I call her when I reach my destination and at the airport in between connecting flights. We talk every day while I'm away. She usually calls me after school though she doesn't always have much to say, just checking in, I think, wanting to hear my voice, to know I'm okay. I've thought about curtailing my absences, finding a way to write without traveling so frequently, searching for that elusive balance.

Over a year ago, I bought an old stone farmhouse to restore. It's a daunting project, having been neglected then abandoned for nearly twenty years and requiring new electricity, plumbing, heating, and windows to make it livable. I've admired the house for the ten years that I've lived in Vermont and the instant I set foot onto its wide-plank floors, I knew it was mine. Despite its dilapidation, I envisioned our furniture scattered about, olive-colored walls in the dining room, an inviting fire in the kitchen, a beautiful place for Alex and me, a place she can return to during college breaks, with her family someday, a home to pass down the generations.

I am thrilled with the restoration's progress, having found a skilled and sensible builder, and my excitement about moving in intensifies with each visit. Yet I'm rarely on site, once a week at most. There's no need, I reason, the contractor's in control, and the writing deadlines continue to mount, but I wonder if there's something more that keeps me away, some underlying reticence about laying down roots as thick as the ledge beneath the house.

"You won't be the same person when you come home," my mother speculated in a moment of calm about the impending trip. I had been thinking the same thing. We talked about the poverty and despair I was likely to encounter, avoiding the potential dangers I might as well. Naturally, she was distressed about my going and her anxiety-management techniques spanned the range of traditional defense mechanisms. Initially, she had e-mailed me a litany of reasons I shouldn't go, starting with the one that resonated most.

"You have a daughter. Alex needs you."

I stared at the computer monitor for a long while, volatile emotions brewing—anger, guilt, doubt, resolution, more anger.

Didn't she know that I knew that? That I lay awake at night wondering myself why I was going? That I worried about leaving my only child motherless?

"I'm not stupid. You need to let me live my own life." Send.

More recently, she had reverted to humor, a defense mechanism of the highest order, according to a friend, and one our family routinely employs. Knowing I was going to Sudan with an Irish relief organization, she joked, "Maybe you should dye your hair red, start practicing your Irish brogue"—a nod to the post-9/11 reality that Americans are targets abroad.

We continued to manage our anxieties through humor, but privately those three words—*Alex needs you*—ran laps through my head.

When you become a parent you inherit society's inclination to judge, and the weight of collective condemnation comes crashing down with each seemingly inconsequential and personal decision—what you pack them for lunch, if you tolerate their tantrums, how much allowance you give them. As a single mom who's away often, I don't stand a chance of passing society's deep-rooted, rigid standards.

"Where will Alex stay?" they inquire nonchalantly, many fully aware of our joint custody arrangement.

What they really want to ask is, "Why aren't you staying home with her?"

The night before I leave for Africa, Alex and I occupy our usual places in the kitchen: she plopped on a counter barstool, me leaning against the stove. She has read something I've written about Sudan and I'm scanning her face for reactions.

"I know you don't like it when I travel," I try to console her.

"No, it's not that . . . " she trails off, emotions clutching her voice. She takes out the article and points to the section about the perils of traveling to Sudan. I inhale deeply and move back toward my spot in front of the range, wondering how to traverse this tightrope of honesty. Her eyes moisten. She waits.

"I'll be fine," I finally say.

"How can you be sure of that?" She calls my bluff.

"Well, I can't," I admit, "but I've got to tell myself that. And so do you."

The words slowly settle into the room like soft rain collecting in shallow puddles along the road.

Eventually, she makes her way upstairs for bed and I follow. We are both plaintive, the trip looming over us in heavy resignation. Climbing into bed, she puckers her lips in a faux pout and we laugh, a welcome interruption to the evening's solemnity. I sit down on the bed next to her.

"I'm gonna miss you so much," I say, giving her a hug. Her lithe, flannel-clad body feels tiny in my embrace.

"I'm gonna miss you, too," she offers.

"Want me to lie down next to you?"

"Sure."

She lets me snuggle up beside her like I did when she was younger. We talk and giggle for a few minutes, then allow the silent night to creep in. I stare at the glow-in-the-dark stars on the ceiling, listening to her breath. The exhales slow and deepen as she sinks into sleep. Making my way across the room, I'm besieged with an unexpected voice. *Don't go.* I gradually open the door. The voice screams louder. *Don't go.* I leave the room, softly closing the door behind me.

* * *

I'm tempted to jump in, but the image of guinea worms painfully inching out of my skin twelve months after gestation keeps me squarely on the muddy bank. The river of coffee stretched before me is not particularly enticing, but the temperatures have been pushing 125 degrees since we arrived. The first full day in Sudan, I crashed for three hours in my hut, thoroughly immobilized by the midday heat. Lately, we've taken to evening strolls along the river when the heat subsides and the light softens.

"*Cai bak,*" I call to the children.

They laugh heartily, pleased at my novice attempt to speak Dinka. Bobby brings out his video camera. Hunching low, he aims at a young woman's ankles as she walks home from the market, the kids shrieking with amusement at this westerner's puzzling ways. Walking and glancing cautiously behind her, she tolerates Bobby's presence for a dozen full strides before fleeing, clearly bewildered by his apparent foot fetish. Our trusted Sudanese guide and translator, Rehan, and I howl; a chorus of innocent giggles follows.

Down by the river, the young children gather around us like dew to petals. A frail little boy with doe eyes comes into Bobby's frame. He is barefoot and wears a tattered pair of blue shorts exposing one side of his buttocks. Though he's probably six, his upper arms are the size of my wrists. As Bobby clicks frame after frame, the boy looks at him sheepishly, idly fondling a piece of elephant grass. Turning my way, his face inches into a coy smile. I can't take my eyes off him.

I ask Rehan his name.

"Duong," he replies. "Rehan," Bobby calls out from behind the lens. "This little guy is so thin. He needs to go to the feeding center, don't you think?"

Rehan examines Duong and agrees. "I'll make sure he gets to the clinic," he says.

A strong, intelligent man, Rehan fled Khartoum, Sudan's capital, in 1998 when the fundamentalist Islamic regime began forcing university students into military training. Rather than fight against his tribe in the south, Rehan risked a more immediate death by attempting to escape. He arrived back home twenty-eight days later to crippling famine. Each Sunday during the height of the drought, he slaughtered one of his bulls, the Western equivalent of burning currency, to feed the villagers.

Bobby has shifted his focus to a small child clad in an unwashed tan frock. A traditional Dinka necklace draped around her small neck, the girl sits patiently on the riverbank, allowing him to snap repeated photos. She looks at him impartially, neither posing nor retreating, her face conveying only the slightest hint of an unexpected pleasure in his attention. Like a seasoned model, she maintains a relaxed gaze, staring intently into the lens, compliantly looking away when he gestures for her to do so.

Rehan and I sit further up the bank, watching Bobby work and enjoying the tranquility of the closing day. A teenage boy methodically zig-zags downriver in a dugout canoe, a lanky, dark figure in relief against a hazy sky. Standing in the bow of the canoe, he gently dips the palm frond paddle into the water, one side, then the other.

Click, click, click. Bobby is riveted to the girl.

"How many photos of one person does Bobby need to take?" Rehan asks mischievously.

His humor is rewarded with a playful shove and a wide smile and our laughter floats down the riverbank in gentle, undulating waves. And it occurs to me that this is what I will remember about Sudan. This, right here by the river. The laughter. The amber wash of the receding African sun. The children. The muddy river. The boy paddling the dugout canoe. The dignity and courage of the Dinka people.

The last of the evening light seeps out across the plains as a sliver of orange candy drops behind the horizon. We walk back to the compound, children at our heels. The little girl of Bobby's photo shoot walks beside me and slips her hand into mine. I smile down at her, touched by the affection. We stroll contently for a bit, then I feel her hand ease away. Walking toward her family's compound, she bids me a parting smile.

Lying in bed later that night, I am seized with a crushing, dreadful feeling, a seed planted the first evening in the compound: I have no desire to go home. I know I will, of course, because of Alex. But only because of Alex, I feel.

I probe the unconscious longings that draw me to this inaccessible land, that grab hold of me, refusing to let me walk away unscathed. What nourishes such an intense desire to stay? A naive fantasy to save the world? A profound sense of purpose in helping others less fortunate? Knowing I can't stay? I ponder the endless stream of silent questions with imperceptible answers but cannot cradle the one question I fear most: What will happen to these generous and joyful people?

The thumping of drums and chants emanates from down near the river, an almost nightly ritual of indescribable shrills and hollow echoes. Like cardiac rhythms, the pulsating beat finally carries me to sleep.

"That's it," says Collins of the engine drone above.

Bags packed, emotions braced for departure, we've been anticipating the plane all morning. As the Buffalo circles overhead, I hop into the back of the Land Cruiser one final time for the short ride to the airstrip. Lazarus, Rehan, and some of the other Sudanese aid workers pile in. Others, on foot, make their customary trek to greet the plane, pulled magnetically toward the implied hopefulness of the swath of dirt. The small craft swoops in low and sputters to a stop, wildly resurrecting dust from the parched earth. Justus, one of the Kenyan aid workers, helps me unload the luggage from the back of the pickup. Turning toward him to say goodbye, I feel tears pooling in the rims of my eyes. Oh, God, not now, not here. Fearful of deteriorating into a sobbing mess, I shove on my sunglasses and look away.

Throngs of barefoot, scrawny kids, some barely clothed, surround the plane. I'm surprised to see little Duong from the river.

"Hi Duong," I say warmly, touching his tiny arm.

"You know his name," Lazarus says, with a blend of inquiry and astonishment.

"Of course," I reply, returning his smile.

Still grasping his arm, I gently pull Duong towards Lazarus.

"Lazarus, he's so thin. He needs to come to the feeding center," I implore. "How come he's so thin?"

"There's nothing to eat," explains Lazarus in a half-chuckle that projects a good-natured incredulity at my ignorance, still, after three weeks in this desolate place.

An organized chaos swirls about the airstrip. Villagers return home, others pointlessly queue for a ride to safety. One pilot checks the manifest, while teenage aid workers help the other one refuel the plane from a blue steel drum. Rehan directs the Sudanese staff to bring the arriving supplies to the compound.

I've been delaying this farewell, its finality ripping at my every fiber. Desperate to conceal my intense sadness, I offer brief hugs and firm handshakes. I'm the last one to board the plane. It is stifling hot, crammed with people and bags. A wrenching ache engulfs me. Tears and sweat drip freely down my cheeks in hot, sloppy streaks. Unable to watch the beautiful black faces—and all they have come to signify to me—fade into the harsh landscape, I stare out the scratched Plexiglas of the aircraft's right side toward the plains and watch the dirt and the river and the grasses disappear into a blanket of brown.

Thirty thousand feet above the Atlantic, I am in a strange place, longing to be in two distinct worlds, occupying neither. I anticipate a challenging re-entry, wondering through what modified lens I will view my post-Sudan world. It is the first time since leaving for Africa that I intensely miss Alex, and the cravings for her physical presence percolate inside me like they have on previous journeys.

Slammed with jet lag and lack of sleep, I am crashed on the couch when she walks through the door looking an inch taller, but with the same sweet smile widening across her face. Tossing my arms around her, I am relieved to see her again. I show her the spears and the Dinka beads I brought back from Sudan. It's late, so we head up to bed.

"Snuggle with me tonight," I say.

"Okay," she says.

Crawling under the flannel sheets we each lie on our sides facing away from the window. We move closer to each other.

"Great to see you again, sweetie," I say, slinging my arm over hers.

"Yeah," she whispers.

My exhaustion draws me further into the mattress. Not

wanting to be in one place, missing the other, I breathe in deeply and release a prolonged sigh, chasing away the intense memories of Sudan.

Tonight, I want to be home.

I traverse two worlds, one represented by the wall-sized map at the travel clinic, the other by after-dinner Yahtzee games and a rambling old stone house, struggling to reconcile the strong desire for family with my unrelenting urge to roam, experiencing life in its unfettered randomness.

Ketchup and Convertibles

by Karen Ackland

We're driving to the camp store—my husband, Larry, his two daughters, and me—to buy ketchup. I think it's unnecessary to drive an hour for a bottle of ketchup, but then, I'm not the one who wants it.

Examining the ice chest this morning, Alexis and Jennie discovered that I planned to barbecue pork chops for dinner. I needed ketchup, they told me. But these pork chops have been marinating in homemade teriyaki sauce and don't need ketchup, I replied. The girls informed me that they always have ketchup with pork chops. They can't eat pork chops without ketchup. Besides, I didn't bring enough Pepsi.

This is the second time we've gone camping over the Fourth of July. Last year, when we were getting to know each other, the girls suggested camping, to the surprise of their father. They are suburban kids, accustomed to malls and fast food, but they assured him they love camping. I suspected they considered their father and me too inept to manage a relationship without their help and thought sleeping together in a tent would move things forward.

This year their father are I are safely married, and the girls have progressed from wooing to indoctrinating. They've become teenagers, and I'm on my way to becoming a mom.

"Look at the purple lupine," I say, riding shotgun. "Maybe we'll come back and hike around the volcanic area tomorrow." Occasionally, my husband glances in the direction I am pointing, but the two in the back are hooked up to portable CD players. The only sound I hear is a faint clicking as they repeatedly listen to the same phrase over and over again. I'm not sure why this should bother me, but I wish they'd play the thing all the way through.

I am momentarily encouraged that Alexis looks up, until she yells as if she's gone suddenly deaf, "I'm not going up there."

"On your life," Jennie adds, not recognizing that she, too, is shouting.

"Boring."

I feel like a tour guide on a geriatric bus.

When we reach the small camp store, the girls spring into action. Besides ketchup, they need Hershey's chocolate milk, vanilla wafers, a giant jar of cheese dip, tortilla chips, and, of course, Pepsi. Normally I try to avoid processed foods, but feeling powerless to curtail the flood of junk food, I buy myself a box of licorice whips.

I dole out quarters for the public showers located behind the store. Arriving last night, the first thing the girls did was check out the restrooms. Not finding a shower, they insisted on packing up right then and leaving. This morning, I stopped them from hailing the ranger as he drove through the camp. They had some suggestions for how he could remodel the bathroom.

There is a long line at the showers and I try to convince the girls to perform a minimal toilette. "We're camping," I tell them cheerfully. "We get to go without showers and make-up." I'm given a look that makes me feel like a teenager who's just done something that will permanently prevent popularity.

Back at camp, Larry and I carry the ice chest and four plastic crates filled with cooking supplies from his SUV. For years I went camping regularly with my friend Julie, leaving early Saturday morning for an impromptu weekend away, our cooking supplies thrown together in a single tote bag. It took hours to pack the car for this trip. Every available space inside is filled, a container on the roof overflows with gear. I feel weighted down.

I hoped to convey my own enthusiasm about the outdoors to the girls, the sense of wonder I feel seeing light filtered through the tops of redwood trees or spotting a fawn in a meadow. I remember camping as a girl and marveling at the things my father knew how to do, things that weren't part of our suburban lives. I wanted the girls to see my husband in a similar way. I didn't allow that they might have agendas of their own.

In the next campsite two young women who've recently

arrived in a red Mustang convertible are setting up a backpacking tent and grilling what look like tuna steaks. There are two stemmed glasses on their table and a bottle of white wine. On my table there is a two-liter bottle of Pepsi, chips and salsa, chocolate chip cookies, a can of bug spray, a quart of cream rinse, and a pile of damp towels. I'm feeling decidedly matronly and it's not attractive.

Afraid my staring will be misinterpreted, I say hello to the two women the next time I make a trip to the Jeep. They've gotten off to a late start, but plan to hike Lassen Peak tomorrow. It'll be a struggle for me to coax my group onto the paved walk to the Sulfur Works without their threatening to puke from the smell.

I want to explain to the women that I used to be like them. I want them to know that Alex and Jennie are my husband's children, that I don't like Pepsi, and that, in other circumstances, I'd hike Lassen Peak myself. I want these things to be clear.

Why do I need to explain myself? While the girls may not admit it, we are having a good time. Early in our relationship, the girls discovered that I easily startle, so they've spent much of the last two days hiding in toilet stalls or behind the tent fly, jumping out suddenly to yell, "Boo." I scream; they laugh and run to tell their father.

This morning I cajoled Jennie into taking a hike with me to see the wildflowers. We ended up in a beautiful meadow with sufficient snow to build a miniature snowman. She hadn't enjoyed a single minute, she assured me when we got back to camp, but I recognized that for the negotiating ploy it was.

* * *

I have more experience entertaining myself in a foreign city than amusing two kids in a national park. I've ordered dinner in a different language with more assurance—certainly with more culinary success—than I exhibited the other night when we stopped at Wendy's on our way to the park. Everyone, including my husband, knew exactly what combo meal they wanted by the time we reached the counter, while I frantically tried to read the overhead menu.

When I traveled with a friend, the days would stretch out in unplanned, indulgent ways. We'd sit for hours in cafés reading books and drinking coffee. Or we'd take a long hike and later skip dinner. We didn't consciously avoid families, but we didn't spend much time around them either.

When I did encounter families, I sensed suspicion, or maybe envy, from mothers. Single and childless, I seemed to project an unsubstantiated dislike of children.

"It must be nice to be here by yourself," a mother might sigh. Or I heard numerous versions of the familiar, "You can't understand." I knew that in an important way I couldn't. But empathy never seemed to run both ways.

With or without Alexis and Jennie, my personal appearance is the same, but with two kids beside me, I'm a mom handing out junk food. It is not so much that I've lost my identity; I've assumed another. At forty-five, falling in love, marrying, and becoming a part-time mother was an unexpected gift. But I spent too many years as a single woman to instantly identify with moms.

We all need to declare ourselves, and once again my stepdaughters are taking the lead. They are not the kind who willingly go hiking, eat pork chops without ketchup, or skip their daily showers. They have an easier time defining themselves than I do.

"I used to be like you," I want to tell the young women in the red Mustang. "And now I have kids."

Reconnecting on the Serengeti

by Beth Livermore

*We are trapped in a mud-shackled Land Rover between a seven-*ton elephant and a pool full of hippopotamuses. Slowly but steadily, the bull and his herd plod toward us as hippos burp warnings from behind. My mother, the picture of calm, looks up from our buried wheel at an impressive set of ten-foot-long tusks.

"One day this will make a funny story," she says, smiling.

Sure, I think. Like the one about the angry elephant that trampled a family to death, or the hippo that stamped a man in half for getting a little too close.

By any measure, it was a strange moment to feel suddenly close to my mom. But the situation reminded me of so many other misadventures we'd lived through and laughed about. There was the car whose brakes went out on a Rocky Mountain road, the tanker our sailboat barely outran, the horses we rescued from a busy highway, and, of course, the Thanksgiving I brought "that boyfriend" home. Some women reconnect over long walks and fireside chats. For

Mom and me, it was an eight-day trip to Tanzania. As we reveled in the sight of cheetahs, wildebeest, and a sky big enough to hold four rainbows, we rediscovered the best in each other.

I think both of us were a little surprised to connect that first night at Mount Meru Game Lodge. Just a month before, we'd been on the phone, New York to Cape Cod, talking about Mom's lifelong dream of going to Africa. This was not news; for years she had savored *National Geographic* specials and read books like *Born Free.* But her interest had recently grown stronger. She wanted binoculars for her birthday, a book of photographs of the Serengeti for Christmas, and a camera with a zoom lens for her anniversary. So when I learned that I would be in South Africa on assignment, we put our heads together to make her dream come true.

Choosing to safari in Tanzania was easy.

"We have to go where the most game is," Mom said. "And let's avoid crowds."

Kenya was our first thought, but our outfitter, Illinois-based Abercrombie & Kent, suggested that we consider Tanzania, which lies to the south. Less developed than its famous sister state, it hosts the continent's most diverse group of animals and encompasses the Serengeti Plain, the Ngorongoro Crater, and Kilimanjaro. If we were lucky, the wildebeest migration, one of the world's spectacular natural sights, would occur during our visit.

Soon after the trip started, we knew we'd made a good choice.

* * *

It's the first day. After meeting Alex, our driver, Venance, our guide, and the five other travelers in the group, we lead ourselves into two minivans and set off for Tarangire National Park. All of us are eager to trade the dusty streets and bustling storefronts of Arusha for one of Tanzania's largest game parks. After several hours of red clay roads and pale blue horizons, we encounter twenty enormous pachyderms at the park gate. Like schoolchildren on a first trip to the zoo, we stand hypnotized by their movement, tickled by their size. Inside the park, Thompson's gazelles prance across fields filled with zebras, and doe-eyed giraffes peek out from behind great stands of flat-topped acacia trees. Warthogs snort as they trot over anthills. That night I dream of wild elephants—as I will for the rest of the trip—beneath the sagging eaves of our rain-soaked tent.

The next morning we wake before sunrise for an early game drive. Just minutes into the trip we observe nature at its harshest. "Fresh kill," Venance says, pointing to a brown mound on the horizon. "Let us go and see what is waiting for us." Alex turns the van in the direction Venance's binoculars point. What we find is a pack of hyenas eating their way through a moaning wildebeest. Like a hangman's audience, we are both captivated and horrified. The hyenas thrust themselves deep into their victim's hindquarters to rip free great tangles of intestine. Bloated and bloodstained, they swagger away in the muddy light of dawn. Stringy chunks of flesh hang from their terrifying jowls. The vultures swoop in.

"Survival of the fittest," says Mom, ready to move on to the next sight—and we do.

But those aren't her last words on the subject. Over breakfast she marvels over the laws of nature: so simple, so cruel, so beautiful. Ruminating over a cup of tea, she points out that here in Tanzania we are reminded that nature's patterns are life, not a metaphor for it.

"Here you feel more like an actor than a director in this drama we call destiny," she says.

Pretty philosophical, I think. I'd forgotten that she bothers with such thoughts. But then, it was my mother who taught me to love twilight and the stillness of winter. It was she who made me take notice of fireflies in the springtime, the warmth of summer sand, the crunch of autumn leaves. She has always drunk in meaning along with sights. I'll be reminded of this again at our next stop, Lake Manyara National Park in the Great Rift Valley.

The Lake Manyara area is a patchwork of habitats, a veritable wildlife wonderland. Soft blonde grasslands meet muddy marshes. Dark mahogany forest flattens to hot, itchy scrubland. From a ridge above, a glassy lake glows pink with flamingos. But it is impossible to imagine the rich national treasure that awaits us. Here baboons perch on muscular tree branches that weave themselves into a jungle. Hippos sleep in murky brown pools. Fat-rumped zebras zigzag across the bushveld. At dusk, lightning bursts slash the pastel sky like razors. A bevy of bleach-white ibis draw silver wakes in clear blue pools.

"What a spiritual place," Mom gasps. "It feels like the dawn of man." Indeed, little has changed here since the Pleistocene Epoch. Sitting beside the lake you can hardly avoid the really big questions. How did life on earth begin? Why are we here? Where will we go? Mom and I end up sharing them all. For a moment we pause and think of my sister Sue. She hates any kind of "chatter." "You guys are such saps," she'd say if she were here. And unless we were serving gin and tonics, she would have changed vans hours ago. We laugh. We miss her. Then we go on chattering.

The next day we leave the diverse landscape of Lake Manyara for the arid Serengeti, where the big question of the day is: Which is most spectacular . . . the sky, the plains, the variety of wildlife, or the wildebeest migration? The sky is so vast that you feel as though you're at sea. But the plains are endless; you half expect to see the curve of the earth. And the animals, numbering more than 1.5 million, make up the largest concentration of wildlife in the world. Still, perhaps the most awesome of all is the wildebeest migration.

Your average wildebeest looks like a "cow by committee," quips a fellow traveler. "Individually they are really quite homely," Mom says. The average male stands about four feet tall and has a black mane, rectangular face, billy-goat beard, big muscular chest, and sagging back end. But during the migration when great rippling herds of them rush south from the Masai Mara, they are powerful, purposeful, somehow even handsome. What looked this afternoon like ellipsis dots on the horizon turns into a stream of beating hoofs. The wildebeest run, walk, to the cyclic rhythm of nature. "My god, this is beautiful," says Mom.

That night she flings wide the curtains of our rooms and watches the animals flood into the plains. She hums to the soundtrack of *Out of Africa,* which pipes through her headset, as she memorizes their movements, their patterns, the color of the sky, everything. For the past several years, family illness, death, and the standard trials of life have worn away at my mom. Sometimes, she says, it is even hard to feel. But hearing the excitement in her voice, watching her eyes fill with glee at the sight of the wildebeest, I know that there is plenty of heart left. Plenty of hope, plenty of wonder. "This is so incredible," she says, breathless. "I close my eyes and all I can see is wildebeest."

Our fifth day is more of the same, but better. We start off at 4:30 A.M. with a hot-air balloon ride and champagne breakfast. Floating high above the trees, we eavesdrop on unsuspecting lion prides and buffalo herds. Then, once we've landed, we drink flute after flute of carbonated cheer. At the breakfast table, which sits in the middle of a field with wild zebras wandering in the background, frank talk comes easy. At first Mom speaks about the realities of innkeeping, from which she and Dad have recently retired. But afterward she turns to the challenge of having an adventuresome daughter. She mentions my trip to El Salvador, the story I did in Egypt, my single life in New York City, and skydiving. Until now I've thought little about how my escapades might affect her. She has always encouraged me, rarely warned against my doing anything. After breakfast the group members raise their champagne glasses to the Serengeti. I raise mine to my mom.

Later that day we leave the Serengeti for Olduvai Gorge, the prehistoric excavation site where the Leakey family made its name. We listen to the lecture on the fossils (including footprints) found here in different strata of rock, which establish man's existence as far back as 3.5 million years ago. Then we visit a Masai village. Though it's somewhat contrived, since Abercrombie & Kent routinely drops by with clients, the stop does introduce us to those proud people and their nomadic way of life. I won't soon forget their mud huts, beaded necklaces, and traditional red robes. The day's final destination is the Ngorongoro Crater, where the next morning we'll explore the lost world of the endangered black rhino.

We meet the morning with a mix of excitement and sadness, for this is to be our most spectacular day but also our last. The crater, the largest intact collapsed volcano in the world, measures 150 feet deep and twelve miles wide. It has dramatic scenery and abundant wildlife; in fact, only giraffes, which cannot scale its steep walls, appear to be missing from the scene. Still, the best thing of all is how close you can get to the animals. "Don't you think maybe we should shut the windows?" Mom says as the van pauses less than six feet from a lioness and her cubs. Wildebeest nearly rub up against our fenders. A rhino and her calf, which at first look like rocks, come to life and cross about twenty feet in front of us. We get stuck between an elephant herd and a hippo pool—so close to danger that for a moment we are all too conscious of the frailties dealt us by evolution.

That night, camped cliff-side above the crater, we recount the trip with a greatest hits list. There was the blood-orange Serengeti sunrise, cheetahs on the plains at high noon, and the haunting wildebeest shadows at sundown. Mom pauses mid-thought. "It was a charmed trip. We made our flights, we saw the migration, the weather held out," she says. "That was really lucky," she continues with a sigh so satisfied that it reminds me of her dinner guests after our Christmas feast each year.

But it was much more than that, I think to myself. For, besides executing a successful trip and sharing a grand adventure, we reclaimed common ground that had eroded with separation. And for the first time in years I was reminded of my mom's role in shaping who I've become.

She was, after all, the one who ignited my wanderlust with her own desire to see the Grand Canyon, the Alhambra, and Vermont in autumn. She taught me the rewards of pushing the envelope by going first into a freezing mountain river for the swim of a lifetime. And how often do I repeat her simple, but potent, maxims when I need a kick in the pants? "Don't get lazy. It's the extra effort that makes life worthwhile," says a woman who drove three kids across America in a tent camper to see the country—and thereby changed our lives. "Why not take a chance? You could fall down the stairs and break your neck." I used that one to get on a plane to Antarctica. Still, none of this was apparent until we traveled together as two fully grown women. Now a mother myself, who must constantly choose between safety and opportunity, necessity and whim, I cherish these gifts more than ever.

Escape from Parenting

by Ariel Gore

As soon as I step out of the JFK airport terminal into the muggy dawn, I feel disoriented. It's not that the air is thick with the smells of mildew and rats, although it is. It's not that I am immediately accosted by half a dozen cab drivers, though I am. It's not even that I'm tired and hungover and nauseous after a cheap red-eye flight across the country. No, my confusion this morning has more to do with the new identity zone I am stepping into than with my particular geographical location. I'm on a week-long furlough—I left my seven-year-old daughter back in California—and with only my own feelings to consider, I can't even remember how to make a decision as simple as this: subway or car service?

In Oakland, Maia and I live mostly a quiet life. My hot pink hair and the fact that, at twenty-seven, I am at least a decade younger than most of the other moms at Maia's school hint at a more exciting life than we actually lead. We hang out at Safeway. We feed the cat. I write while Maia is at school. I help her with her homework. She visits her dad. And when I planned to come to New York alone it had more to do with her not wanting to join me than any conscious desire to break away from being "mama." Tillie Olsen wrote that "more than in any other human relationship, overwhelmingly more, motherhood means being instantly interruptible, responsive, responsible." Much has been said about the identity crisis we experience as new mothers. But what happens after we have grown accustomed to our Mamaness? Even comfortable with it? What happens after years of always being interruptible? After we've designed our lives and trained our senses to be always responsive and responsible, what happens when we suddenly land, alone, at JFK and realize that no one really cares how we get to Manhattan?

I end up in a taxi, and I am still a little queasy when I finally get to my friend's apartment on the Lower East Side. I ring his doorbell once and then curl up in his doorway, using the Hello Kitty duffel bag I borrowed from my daughter as a pillow. I probably should have tried harder to wake him, but it's been ages since I rested like this in a doorway, and for the first time in seven years, I can.

It is still early morning, and few people are out on the street. A woman approaches me cautiously and leans down to ask if I need a fix.

"You OK?" she wants to know. "'Cause we can go see my man Raul."

When I wake up I feel youth-sick, and oddly exhilarated. I ring my friend's doorbell and when he hears I've been outside since sunrise he looks at me with a mixture of pity and concern.

"Have you lost your mind?"

I just laugh. I can't say that I haven't.

On this first day, I am cautious. My first book is being published in the spring and I have several business meetings and expense-account lunches to focus on. And although (according to my friend, Dave) I look like a cross between a rock star and a housewife, by my standards, I am dressed up. I amuse myself uttering simple sentences: "Sure, I'll have another beer"; "If I don't come back tonight, I'll just see ya tomorrow"; and, my favorite, "No, I have no interest in going to see the Statue of Liberty." (When I was here with Maia last year, we were poster children for New York tourism—$20 T-shirts and all.)

On the second day, I am giddy. I stop by an old boyfriend's apartment at random hours to have sex—mostly for the thrill of not having to listen for the pitter-patter of little footsteps coming down the hall. He's a guy I lived with in wilder days—when he was in high school and I was the mod party-girl dropout. Now when I scream in his bed I all but forget that he's a Narcotics Anonymous convert and I'm on the PTA.

I call Maia to check in, half-hoping that she will offer me something to feel guilty about, or at least some grounding thoughts. But she doesn't. She hates the city. She is glad she didn't have to come. It's dark in New York, she says, and stinky. She is having a blast with her father, the tooth fairy brought her five bucks and she doesn't need a thing from me.

This isn't the first time in seven years that we've been apart, but I've always stayed in Oakland when Maia went off with her dad for weekend visits. And when I'm on home turf, the circle I travel in is, admittedly, a maternal ghetto. Most of my friends in Oakland have children, so even when I do not have my own baby sitter to relieve, I find myself rushing home from concerts as if my Honda is on the verge of turning into a pumpkin. I spend the days when she is gone catching up on work, and even when I go out to Club Red, I leave before last call. I only stop for one drink after a k.d. lang show. At home I remain in mama-mode: always prepared to respond to an urgent telephone call, checking my messages at least twice a day and rarely allowing my blood alcohol level to creep above the legal limit.

By Thursday, I begin to lose track of days and nights all together. I am often tipsy, but mostly I'm high on the uninterruptedness of it all. I am mesmerized by the flow of time and events—one thing leads to another and another and another—and even when I stop long enough to eat a piece of pizza, no paper airplane noses onto my plate to bring me back to reality. Skidding into adolescent oblivion, I get a CD-sized tattoo on my shoulder at a shop where they blare Violent Femmes like it's 1985. I fall head-over-heels in love with a woman I barely know. A woman with henna in her hair. At a dinner party, someone asks if my daughter knows I will be coming home with the tattoo, and I remember that when I got my first one at sixteen, someone asked if my mother knew.

At 1 A.M. in New Jersey, after an Ani DiFranco show I hear that the trains have stopped running and it doesn't even occur to me to worry about how I'm going to get back to Manhattan. Without a little kid whining about our predicament, without any babysitter to relieve, I have time to wait for luck to kick in. I get back. Of course I get back. I hitch a ride with a busload of crazy Brits who came all the way to the East Coast to see Bob Dylan scratch out a few tunes after Ani left the stage. I stay up until 6 A.M. blaring music and smoking with a friend in her elegant apartment on the Upper West Side. I sleep until noon. I forget to eat.

One morning—I don't know which one—as I am parting from a new friend after spending all night in her tiny East Village apartment talking about hair dye, Beth Lisick prose poems, and bisexuality, I am filled with a strange feeling of deceitfulness when I realize that this new friend knows I was born under the sign of Cancer, knows that the subway signs in this town always make me think of Lawrence Ferlinghetti poems and knows that I prefer black licorice to red, but knows nothing of my daughter and the left front tooth she lost last week.

That afternoon, I confide my identity crisis to a woman at a bar on the Lower East Side who bears an uncanny resemblance to Nina Hagen.

"You're not regressing," the woman assures me. "This is just life without kids."

"You mean, when people don't have kids, they act like this *all of the time!*" I ask, certain that I've misunderstood.

"And you don't get tired?" I ask, incredulous.

She smiles. "Well," she begins slowly as she orders another drink, "you do get tired, but then you just sleep. And, of course, at some point there are health concerns. And if you've got a job or a career or something . . . "

I just stare at her, trying to imagine what my life would be like without anyone to interrupt me, without having to be responsive, responsible. When I was nineteen and pregnant, I used to joke that I was having a baby to keep myself out of trouble. And now I realize that it was true. Here I thought I'd grown up in seven years, and all I'd done was to find another use for my ability to function without sleep. I wonder what my life would be like without my daughter's all-encompassing presence, and I am somewhat comforted to realize that without the grounding effect she has on me, I'd probably just go get myself knocked up.

Risk

The Wetsuit

by Marcia Barinaga

"I can't wear that in public," my mother wails, "I don't want anyone to see me!"

She sits on the edge of her bed, watching me wiggle into a new black wetsuit with yellow and purple racing stripes. An identical suit lies in a jumble in her lap. She glances down at it warily, patting it with her arthritis-gnarled hand.

We're not big exhibitionists in my family. When I was in high school, I ate my lunch stealthily, sitting behind a billboard in the hallway, because I couldn't stand people's eyes on me when I walked into the cafeteria and searched for a seat. And in that way, among others, I am like my mother.

But now I have shown up for her seventy-second birthday with the surprise of a new wetsuit for an upcoming trip she and I are taking to Hawaii. Mom's never been one to seek out wildlife adventures. On family vacations to the Caribbean when I was a teenager, Dad and I spent hours snorkeling, returning with exciting stories of moray eels, barracuda, and schools of squid.

Mom stayed on shore, claiming that she gets too cold when she snorkles, but I suspected she was also secretly grateful for the excuse to not have to meet those creatures herself.

This time will be different. This trip is for the two of us, and I'm not leaving her on shore. The water in Hawaii is colder than the Caribbean, and most serious snorkelers wear wetsuits.

"You'll fit right in," I tell her, "and you'll be warm enough to really enjoy yourself." I decide not to bring up the creatures right now.

"Oh dear, I hope you won't be disappointed if I decide not to snorkel," she says. "Can you return the wetsuit if I don't use it?"

"Sure I can. But don't worry about that," I say, ratcheting up the enthusiasm in my voice. "I know you're going to want to plunge right in once you see that beautiful bay."

I'm expecting too much, I think. I know I will be crushed if she decides not even to try. Will I be able to hide my disappointment from her?

Mom struggles to push her foot into the suit. "It's too small," she groans. "It will never fit."

"Mom, that's not the leg, it's the sleeve!" We dissolve into giggles like overtired kids at a slumber party.

Soon Mom's got the suit on and I've pulled up the long back zipper, gently tucking in the cotton camisole she now wears instead of a bra. The suit hugs the curves of her body like those figure-control bodysuits in the Victoria's Secret catalog. Standing side by side looking in the mirror, I admire the curve of her hips, the trim appearance of her upper arms and shoulders. I note that she is no longer my height. Her hands reach up involuntarily and smooth the skin below her eyes, but she seems pleased with the overall effect.

"Do you think we'll see moray eels?" she asks, her nose crinkling.

"Maybe. But they'll be hiding in the coral, and they won't hurt you," I say.

"I don't think I want to see one," she says with finality.

On our first day in Hawaii, I know Mom is self-conscious walking to the beach past sun worshippers staking out the best beach chairs. But she makes a good show of pretending she's been doing this all her life—snorkel, mask, and fins in one hand, wetsuit draped casually over her shoulder. We stop to admire the beach, a wide crescent of white sand.

"What a ridiculous thing for an old lady to be doing!" she whispers in my ear, conspiratorially. Her eyes shine with excitement.

We pull on our wetsuits, with no blunders this time, thanks to our practice session. We wade in. The water is cool and colorless, "clear as gin," as Mom used to say on our Caribbean vacations. The tiniest of ripples lap softly against the beach. Our feet protruding from the black legs of our wetsuits look strangely pale under water; dots of light dance across them looking like ephemeral silver coins. We don Lycra swim caps—to keep our hair from floating in front of our eyes, I explain—and fit our masks onto our faces. I check hers to make sure the strap is tight, and then show her how to float face down in the water to put on her fins. She's pleased to know the right way to do it, remembering the man in St. Thomas who paraded down the beach in his fins, looking like a high-stepping duck.

We're in a wide bay. "The coral reef is over there, Mom," I say, gesturing, "and the best reef is out where you see those big rocks sticking up."

She looks at the rocks, several hundred feet away. "Oh, I don't know," she says. Her voice reverberates comically through the snorkel she's already fitted into her mouth. She pulls the snorkel out.

"That looks too far. I may want to stay closer to the beach," she confesses.

We float out from the beach, and in a few minutes, I pop up to look around. Mom's headed for the rocks. Her fins churn steadily, like the paddles of a steamboat, and little "ooh"s echo out of her snorkel. Her rear end sticks up a bit, waddling from side to side as she kicks. It looks irresistibly cute. I swim after her.

"Did you see that black-and-purple fish?" she sputters when I catch up with her at the rocks. "It was so beautiful. I tried to follow it, but it swam away!"

For the next hour we float on the bay, like hawks soaring effortlessly on an updraft, surveying the landscape below us. Canyons and mountains of coral fill our view, yellow and green in the sunlight. Big green-and-lavender parrotfish attack the coral with their beaks, making abrupt chomping sounds, and occasionally discharging fine sand as they swim. I show Mom the surgeon fish, black with bright orange scalpel-like blades protruding near their tails. An octopus skulks along the bottom, keeping an eye on us and trying to camouflage himself among the corals. Mom recoils a bit from the sight.

After an hour, I'm ready to head back, starting to feel cold even in my wetsuit. I notice a big green sea turtle hovering behind Mom. She is oblivious to the turtle, intently studying something I can't see. I stop and watch, worried that she will panic when she notices the turtle so close to her. Instead her eyes grow wide inside her mask, and she doggedly follows the turtle toward the shore.

Back in the shallows, after the turtle has swum off, we sit on the sandy bottom, Mom bursting with stories like a seven-year-old.

"I like to pick one fish and follow it," she says, "to see what they do and how they live. I followed a big flounder that buried himself in the sand and disappeared! And I think I saw a moray eel," she adds darkly. "But I wasn't scared."

I smile at the mask pushed casually up on top of her head, the snorkel dangling by her face like she's been doing this for years.

"You look like Lloyd Bridges," I say, recalling the dashing deep-sea diving star of TV's *Sea Hunt* back in the '50s.

"Oh," Mom answers distractedly, her voice trailing off as she swats the snorkel away from her chin. Her mind is not on how she looks. She gazes out across the bay, as if she can now see past its sparkling surface to the hidden life teeming beneath.

"Let's come back first thing tomorrow morning," she says eagerly.

Unmapped Days

by Martha Molnar

We pack only as much as we need for one night. On the cool blacktop in the parking lot, we lay out all our gear, just as we've seen it in *Appalachian Mountain Club* magazine: stove, headlamp, extra socks, rain jacket, food carefully doled out for each modest meal. Apples, bought at a farmers' market along the Oregon coast, weigh down our pants' pockets.

It's a steep climb to the top of the ridge, and our backs and legs are unaccustomed to the weight of our packs. After four rambling hours, we're at the summit. My daughter, Daniela, and I stand transfixed, feeling tiny under the spreading canopy of giants, caught in unexpected splendor. A single hollowed-out trunk is large enough to offer shelter for two. Far below, the Pacific is silent, stretched out taut, iridescent. A yawning white beach lies empty of people. On the other side is a perfectly round lake, an eye as unruffled and iris blue as my daughter's, as thickly fringed with forest as hers is with lashes.

We look at each other, utter wordless sounds, and dance a little jig. We have come for the shock of the newly beautiful, the discovery of a landscape different from the familiar gentleness of the Northeast, and, above all, the thrill of finding it ourselves.

Two weeks ago, immediately following high-school graduation, Daniela willfully put thousands of miles between herself and everything familiar, leaving her suburban New York friends to search for gainful summer employment, and striking out alone across the continent. After four glorious days and five sleepless nights aboard an Amtrak train, she arrived in San Francisco with the happy prospect of a few more days alone before I, her frantic mother, could join her.

Her teenage angst, a simmering anger at a terribly imperfect world, seemed to have subsided by the time we met up. The world's iniquities appeared remote without regular newspapers and National Public Radio news. As we headed north from San Francisco, the scenery along Route 1 became progressively wilder. Our escapes from the car took us mostly to state and national parks, still silent and empty in early June. The ravaged land we had expected appeared amazingly unspoiled, the clearcuts invisible, the pollution scattered by ocean breezes.

Lost in the exhilaration of the new, my "so annoying" parenting became less so. While at home my concerns about my wild daughter's safety seemed so unfounded to her, she was forced to share some of my misgivings here in the wild. Conversations at home consisted of low-level debates, with me maintaining a staunch realism in the face of her untried idealism. But in the unbounded space of open air, our talks flowed easily, focused on each day's simple decisions and shared enjoyment: where to stop for a scenic lunch, in which direction to start the circular hike, whether the firs appeared black against the blue or a very deep green. Our similar sense of humor, our equal willingness to take on physical challenges and accept deprivation for the sake of adventure, our passion for exotic food and music, and especially our shared ecstasy at nature's beauty turned into a source of easy companionship on the road.

In this state of harmony, I didn't want to remind her that we'd never backpacked before, never slept outdoors—except the night before, surrounded by campers with multiple hookups in a cement tundra off Oregon's Interstate 5—that we had struggled for much longer than the five minutes we were promised it would take to put up the tent, that we had never made a fire, not even in the fireplace at home, because that was father's and brothers' work.

Now, like children playing house, we set to work. Sliding on our backsides to the lake, we bring water back to camp to purify it, a simpler task than I'd imagined. Pitching the tent is more complicated, however. On the soft ground, in full view of both ocean and lake, we unroll the flapping cloth. I am once again lost among the metal poles, struggling to line them up according to the confusing instructions. Seeing my frustration, Daniela takes charge and assigns me the easy task.

"Just open the poles and string them through the loops," she instructs coolly. I can do that, I reason, relieved. As I hold up the interior, she swiftly does whatever it takes outside and turns the floppy nylon into a taut shelter.

I congratulate her profusely, truly impressed, but she shrugs it off.

"It's really simple," she notes, fixing me with those large unblinking eyes, clearly at ease being in charge.

"What's a home without a hearth?" I ask, eager to move beyond the tent. The fallen wood around us is heavy with dampness. But the beach is gleaming in midday sun, and likely to be littered with dry, light driftwood. We find a narrow path down the steep sand dune.

"It looks like an animal path," she notes, her tone a mixture of inquiry and declaration.

"Maybe," I answer noncommittally.

"What animals do you think use it?" she continues.

"Probably bears," I answer.

She stops and turns around. A ray of fear shines in her confident eyes.

"Maybe only rattlesnakes," I say mischievously, remembering her early and abiding horror of reptiles. Then, my supremacy restored, I add, unnecessarily, "just kidding, just kidding."

The beach stretches on, white, still, devoid of human footprints. It's littered with giant driftwood in fantastic shapes, monstrous redwood trunks carried away, carved by waves and re-deposited on this sandy sculpture park. We walk several miles, examining the horned lions, the winged turtles, the Easter Island heads, running hands over their smooth lines, sitting in their concave interiors. Digging our feet into the rough sand, the frigid water drains all sensation from our legs, useless columns we haul out to dry in the sun. Nearly dozing on a driftwood lounger, my stomach rumbles and I remember our purpose. Quickly, I call Daniela to order and we begin gathering wood, filling our arms with more than we can carry.

We have long since lost the path back to camp. Searching above the steep face along the ridge, some 400 feet high, yields no clues. My chest tightens.

"It would have been logical to mark the spot," she says. We deposit the driftwood, this time marking the spot with a tall mast, and wander off in opposite directions. Giving up at about the same time, we return to our jumbled pile. I decide we'll bushwhack back to camp. She nods and follows me.

Worn out from counterbalancing the shifting sands, my legs and arms exhausted and aching, I get sloppy and begin dropping the wood. After several stops to rearrange my bundle, she looks at my distraught face, silently picks up the fallen pieces and adds them to her bundle, carrying them without a word. Gratefully, I follow her long, strong legs as we haul ourselves up the last incline and see the tent through the tree trunks.

After a short rest, we boil water on the camp stove and pour it into instant soup, butter bread, prepare tea, and carry everything to the edge of our mountain. Perched like ravens on the cliff's edge, we're at the focal point of the universe. The sun sits on fiery shafts. As we wolf down our dinner, the shafts shorten, dropping the sun into the water. Shadows roll over the ocean like a scroll. We peer across the chasm of darkness, listening closely to the sea of silence.

This is the right time to put a match to the cylindrical bonfire we have prepared. But she reminds me about the food, and about the bears—or maybe just squirrels, I note magnanimously. Yes, I have read that food must be hung, and we have rope and bags to hang from one of the tall trees. But unlike our low-hanging oaks at home, easily climbed, these evergreens are tall and unreachable. How to get the rope high enough off the ground without climbing the tree? We toss the weightless rope up, but it only falls back down at our feet pathetically. I don't recall instructions for this task.

I figure we must tie something heavy to the rope to make it fly. She agrees, and after several failed attempts with pieces of wood, she closes in on a rock.

"How," I ask, "do you intend to tie a rope around a rock and have it stay there while you hurl it?"

Undeterred, her clever fingers fashion a cage of twine around a small rock, which she successfully slings over a branch. Our food bag is hanging some twelve feet up.

"That's too high even for the largest grizzly," she declares with satisfaction.

Now it's finally time. With just a few matches, our little pyramid blossoms, tiny sparks flying from its tongues. The light smoke, sweetened with cones and blackening marshmallows, tickles my nostrils. For at least ten minutes, every pore on my skin opens to the warmth and light.

"We're pretty good, aren't we?" I ask, and she agrees wholeheartedly as we bask in pride and warmth.

The needles and twigs are quickly consumed and the fire becomes an anemic shadow of its blazing self. Our hard-won driftwood refuses to cooperate, barely becoming scorched. We scamper around in the dark, gathering more needles, more twigs, and with each handful the fire flares for a minute or two, then begins to wither.

A stiffening breeze lifts the shirt off my back.

"Do you think it might rain?" she asks.

"Not a chance," I assure her, utterly unsure.

The darkness thickens, amassing a weight that presses onto my bare limbs. The stillness of the afternoon has lapsed into a silence that echoes in my ears. If others are camped anywhere within miles, maybe they don't bother making campfires. Or maybe we're completely alone.

Our fire finally expires in a tiny twist of smoke and a heap of glowing rubies. This is the crucial hour.

"I can't believe no one else is camping in such a perfect place," she says. Her voice is very small in the enormous emptiness around us.

"Are bears attracted to fires or are they afraid of them?" she asks.

"No bears here," I lie with complete confidence. "They never live near oceans."

"But they do in Alaska!" she corrects.

"Those are polar bears, and we're not in a polar region, right?"

No debate here. We establish that no polar bears live within thousands of miles of us. We kill whatever embers remain to mock us, and retreat to the tent.

The sleeping bags retain a bit of the sun's heat and for a little while I feel snug and safe. But the wind—of course it's the wind, right?—whips up a cacophony of unfamiliar noises, fledglings falling out of nests, dry limbs crashing, a tsunami forming, needles and leaves shifting.

"Maybe we should take turns sleeping," she offers.

"Okay, if that makes you feel better. You sleep first and I'll wake you in two hours," I lie again.

I wake in the predawn light to rummaging noises. A bear? Nothing but thin nylon separates us from the 400-pound beast? Is that its haunch I feel brushing the side? Adrenaline surges. The backs of my arms tingle. My throat aches with dryness.

Frozen, I lie very, very still, and the rummaging noises stop.

No pounding footsteps leaving either. Maybe it was just a squirrel, making inappropriately loud sounds.

Still, it is impossible to sleep. I lie saucer-eyed as bear stats crowd my brain. There are some half a million black bears in North America. They almost never attack unprovoked, but there are always exceptions.

It's too dark to read, too cold to leave the bag. I lie still and listen for more rummaging noises. Instead, birds begin to pepper the air with song, my signal to move.

The tent zipper wakes Daniela. One eye flies open then promptly shuts.

Outside, the world seems to have grown purer, sharper while I slept. The redwoods, like the spires of medieval cathedrals, are talking to the pale heavens. The ocean's curve reaches further around, turning our mountain into a tiny spit of land, a tall island in a sea of air. I breathe deeply, exhaling pride, inhaling wonder, exhaling vivid air, inhaling unbounded space. Surely, on the other side of the mountain, a full sun must be rising to make this day as perfect as the last.

But at the moment, the chill is making my nose drip; my numb fingers are aching for a hot cup of coffee to hold. Our food bag is intact, out of reach of bears—and out of my reach too. Had we ever considered how to get the bag down?

I long desperately for the abominable instant coffee. Peering into the tent, I see that Daniela's sleeping on her back, arms flung up, just as she did in babyhood, and my heart goes slack. I can't wake her in this state of innocence. This means no coffee for hours. Dejected, I go sit by last night's damp embers, pull my hat down further, shove my hands into pockets, and wait for the sun. I can't tell if the sky is cloudy or a predawn gray.

Fretting about rain, salivating for bad coffee, I nevertheless doze, and when I wake, the spreading sunrise is reaching up to the trunks, nosing into the open tent door.

"Brilliant daughter," I call, knowing her burrowing deeper is a vain attempt. "I've been awaiting your aid all these long hours. Release my coffee, now!"

Once I put on my glasses I can see just how simple it would have been to get at the coffee, but I let her lower the bag, and indulge her tolerant gaze.

The day that unfolds is dazzling, filled with the promise of long, free hours for body and mind to wander. Overcome with the power and glory of having survived the night, we consider staying another.

I do raise one feeble objection.

"We don't have enough food," I venture. "We only have the rancid cheese, a can of sardines, bread and peanut butter."

"And tea, and coffee," she adds, as if these were calorie-laden meals. "Oh, and cookies."

"Oh, all four of them," I note dryly.

"We'll be fine. It's already almost lunch, so only a few hours to go before we sleep."

I'm the adult, I tell myself, and not one to ignore hunger. I could argue convincingly, and she'd give in. Then we'd slip back into the careful tolerance, the polite exchanges we both maintain to keep from the adversarial positions her friends and mine have with their mothers and daughters. The idyllic harmony of the past few days, born of our equality in the wild, would vanish. With the coffee still gently warming my insides, it's easy to agree that we may, after all, have enough food for just one more day.

We repeat the foray for wood, now taking our time on the way to the beach to examine the rich vegetation. During the many hours on the train, she read books on the natural history of the Northwest, and now proceeds to regale me with a stream of fascinating facts about red cedar and Douglas fir, Western hemlock and Sitka spruce. As we pass on to the pine and shrub—covered hills and grassy knolls, I learn about the invasive European beachgrass, and the sensitive Oregon bog anemone, the pink sand verbena and the bugbane. Near the water we spot what looks to me like any plover, but I stand corrected: it's the threatened western snowy plover.

In my garden and the woods behind our house, I taught her what I knew of the local flora and fauna. I now see how the seed I planted has sprouted and ripened into a dazzling flower, far surpassing my own humble knowledge.

Before we hit the beach, we tie a red and a purple bandana to the shrubs on either side of the path. At lunchtime, they wave us cheerfully back to camp.

But lunch is not enough, and neither is the measly dinner. I'm not actually hungry, but my stomach feels light, my limbs lack energy. I think of John Muir, who walked for weeks with just bread and tea, satiated by the Sierras' unfolding marvels. I think of Edward Abbey living on beans and muddy Colorado water, nourished by adventure. Then I suggest we finish up the cookies.

"Mom, you know they're our only breakfast, and we'll need energy to pack out, not to sleep," she explains, assuming I don't know the facts as well as she does.

"We'll make it somehow, knowing food is waiting at the car," I counter.

"But that'll be hours after we wake up," she says patiently. "We'll be weak without any starch."

I agree in principle, but can't get those dry cookies off my mind. Seize the moment, I think. I need them now.

We read, write, plan another fire. We watch the sun dip into the ocean, same place, same time, and a show as shockingly beautiful as the last. Afterwards, she leaves for our peeing spot and I see my chance. My mouth is actually watering.

I can't find them. Shocked and embarrassed, I realize she's taken the cookies with her. I retreat to the small fire.

"So what kinds of bears live around here?" she asks nonchalantly.

Now it's my turn to shine. I recite the relevant bear facts I've gleaned from my own reading, carefully staying away from the drama of the rare attacks. Then I move from earthbound bears to the starlit sky, and together we search for the Milky Way, the North Star, the Big Dipper.

The darkness shrinks our world to the small flame. She moves her rock closer to mine, and I put my arm around her. Leaning gratefully against me, a tremulous sigh escapes her. Every few minutes she swivels her head around, peering into the opaque air, thinking of bears. I tighten my grip on her shoulder and talk about the stars.

Beyond the Portage

by Susan Catto

It is possible to travel from one end of Canada to the other entirely by canoe, a symbol of wilderness and adventure, iconic as beer and maple syrup, and the main form of transportation for native tribes and European traders for centuries. Yet somehow I'd managed to grow up in Canada without learning to canoe. In fact, I could not even remember riding in a canoe, an admission greeted with incredulity by my Canadian friends, all veterans of summer camp and trips to lakeside cottages. Even my mother, a Michigan native, had learned to canoe at age sixty-five, joining an Elderhostel trip on the French River near Sudbury just months after obtaining Canadian citizenship.

I decided to rectify my unpatriotic lapse with a three-day canoeing trip in Algonquin Park, a pristine preserve with 930 miles of interconnected canoe routes between Toronto and Ottawa. I asked my mother, Helen, to join me.

She and I were seasoned travel companions. We had explored Scotland by train and England by bus. We had braved a frigid two weeks on the Turkish coast during the coldest April in forty years, and had been stranded in Rhodes, Greece, when I misread the departure time on the ferry. While trips with friends and partners succeed or fail based on how well we get along or how much each of us likes our destination, I can embark on any trip with my mother confident that we'll have a fabulous time. Both of us possess sufficient optimism and curiosity that the inevitable discomforts and disappointments of travel are a welcome part of the adventure. Sure, we irritate each other sometimes—I was cross with my mother for hours when she made me go back into a Turkish bath in Marmaris to retrieve her shampoo, leading to a mortifying encounter with a local man naked but for soap suds—but any annoyance only lasts until the next mealtime. We both take such delight in tasting new foods that it would seem sacrilegious to go through a meal without exchanging bites and comparing opinions.

But this time, our positive traveling history and my mother's canoeing experience notwithstanding, I assumed she would decline my invitation. She had recently undergone cancer surgery and was regaining her strength after completing chemotherapy. I could imagine her spending the weekend at a spa or a fancy resort, but three days of canoeing and sleeping in tents? To my surprise, she accepted immediately, saying it had been a lifelong dream of hers to canoe in Algonquin Park. There was no time like the present for fulfilling lifetime dreams, she added.

So, on a sunny July day, my mother and I packed the car and headed north. As the city traffic slipped away, so did months of distance between us. In part, I had asked my mom to join me because I missed her. A few years ago, I had moved back home after nearly a decade away at college in New York and graduate school in England. I lived with my mother while I finished my thesis and found my first job. For two years, we were constant companions—going to the gym, cooking exotic meals, watching movies, and talking politics. Just before my mother's cancer diagnosis, I had moved in with my future husband, and between my new life and the chaos of her cancer treatment, our old times together seemed very far away. I think she was eager to join me because she missed me, too.

Together now in the car, we had a chance to talk again about the little things—movies, recipes, and politics. Hours later, after stopping to tour an Algonquin Indian reserve and eat a lunch of stew and bannock, we drove through the gates on the eastern side of Algonquin Park and approached our camp, Northern Edge Algonquin.

Over a vegetarian dinner we met our companions for the next three days. Donna, a dog trainer from Toronto, had canoed before but hadn't camped in decades. Fred, a landscape designer from Michigan, was an experienced paddler who visited Northern Edge every summer. The new-age emphasis and relatively high prices of Northern Edge attract an older crowd, but my mother was still the eldest by twenty-five years. Our guide, Rob—a young and preternaturally tranquil outdoorsman—was tasked with managing our disparate expectations and abilities.

After dinner, Northern Edge staff led the guests in rhythmic drumming around a stone-encircled campfire. I slipped off to the dock to look for loons, whose nightly calls are a reliable lullaby of Algonquin Park evenings. In the twilight, water bugs scooted across the water's surface and lake trout leapt from the lake to feast on shadflies.

We retired to our comfortable cabin and rose the next morning to help pack the canoes. The sky threatened rain, and I was chilly even in three layers of shirts and sweaters. We pushed off the dock with my mother in the bow and me in the stern. Rob taught us the basic sweep and the J-stroke, which, theoretically at least, allows the rear canoeist to keep the boat moving in a straight line.

After nearly an hour of paddling across Kawawaymog Lake, I had almost learned to steer straight. Then Mom and I reached the Amable du Fond, a river that bends and curves like a mountain road. We ran over lily pads, crushed pinecone-shaped purple and white flowers floating on the water's surface, and knocked wild pink roses from their bushes at the river's edge. Marsh grasses gave way to towering forests of spruce, pine, and cedar, but I had stopped looking up, needing all my concentration to maneuver past logs and rocks submerged in the shallow water. Our guide traveled patiently behind us, while the other two canoeists waited for us at the first portage.

"Portage" is a graceful word for a difficult feat. As Rob explained, we would need to unload all the packs, carry them and the canoes over the steep 450-foot path, then load everything back into the boats and continue the journey. Looking at the heap of possessions that needed hauling, I wondered again whether we should have gone to a spa.

The five of us were traveling with three canoes, two stoves, four tents, several large water jugs, five plastic food barrels, sleeping bags, ground mats, and five sets of clothing. I felt as if all of it were stuffed into the giant pack lashed to my back.

And then I looked at my mom, who was herself loaded down with gear. "Do experienced canoeists start to enjoy the portages?" she asked politely, which I knew was her way of asking, "In exactly what way can this torture be considered pleasant?"

Rob laughed. "No one enjoys a portage in itself," he explained. "But since most people would rather avoid them, each portage takes you further from civilization into a more private, untouched part of the park."

When we finished our second portage and entered North Tea Lake, I understood what he meant. It was high season, and the campsites accessible by car had been fully booked for months. Hiking trails near the main West Gate parking lot bustled with day-trippers. In contrast, we saw only two other groups, and they soon vanished behind the islands dotting the lake. The sun finally emerged; the air was sweet and the clear water had a pleasant, slightly metallic scent. We ate a lunch of cheeses and fruit on a tiny island with outcroppings of pink stone and a carpet of wild blueberry plants.

On the final leg of that day's trip, my mother and I switched positions. The wind threw up small waves, and my stronger stroke, coming from the front of the canoe, negated my mother's efforts to steer. The pleasant feeling of achievement we'd had after the portages faded into grim determination as we struggled to cross the choppy water. It was hard to gauge our progress against the constant backdrop of forest, but we were barely moving. I tried to steer from the front of the canoe, switching my paddle from side to side, my hand and sleeve dipping into the waves with every stroke. In the back, my mother looked white-faced and exhausted and I felt sick with regret. I knew the effort was too much for her—it was nearly too much for me—but we had to keep paddling. We were in the middle of the lake and if we didn't inch forward we would be pushed back by the wind. Near tears, we redoubled our efforts.

Finally, more than five hours after setting out, we reached our destination, a little island halfway through North Tea Lake. Algonquin Park is dotted with hordes of back-country campsites, accessible only by boat and available on a first-come, first-served basis. The beauty of our site was some consolation for the arduous journey. A clearing just big enough for our four tents faced a stone-encircled hearth and makeshift benches nailed together by earlier visitors. An upside-down "L" of planks had been nailed to a tree at a perfect height for chopping and serving food. A stand of trees formed a natural frame for the lake, which glinted in the late-afternoon sun. The outhouse was hidden down a path strewn with pine needles.

Even the hard ground couldn't keep me from sleeping soundly that night, and the next day we had the luxury of canoeing from a home base. It was cold and misty once again, and my mother elected to stay at the campsite and read. The rest of us canoed to a hiking trail down the coastline. Wolf and deer droppings were the only signs that non-human creatures had used the path.

By our final evening at the camp, the five of us were old friends. Lacking ghost stories to tell around the campfire, we improvised. Fred read from a book of Toltec philosophy and Donna told us how she used positive reinforcement to train everything from terriers to rabbits. I recounted the plot of my favorite book, Samuel Richardson's lengthy novel *Clarissa*. My mother was relatively quiet. We hadn't mentioned her illness to the others, and she told me afterwards that it had been a pleasure to shed her cancer-patient persona for a few days.

It was sunny and hot as we broke camp the next day. Rob had recognized the folly of putting my mother and me in the same canoe—together, we were twice as slow as the others—so she rode with him and I paddled swiftly along with Donna. We stopped along the way for a swim in the sun-warmed waters.

After being so alone during our stay on the lake, it was a shock to reach the portages and see dozens of people heading deep into the park. It was a reminder that we were returning to reality. After days together in the wilderness, we would return to the city and our everyday lives.

I was proud of my mother. She had much to complain about: a deadly disease, surgeries, a long recovery, and a discouraging prognosis. Yet I never heard her lament her situation, much less bemoan the little discomforts so common in the wilderness. Her strength was inspiring. Perhaps the trip was so moving because we suspected it might be our last. That apprehension, however, was unstated, and, as it has turned out, untrue. In a year when so much had been taken away, we had given each other the gift of time and love.

Distance

Together Apart

by Jessica Hoffmann

Shortly before my mother and I are scheduled to leave for a twelve-day trip to Peru, she calls to wonder aloud if this might not be more her kind of trip than mine, if it's really the right thing for us to do together. But I'm committed, we're going, I brush her concerns aside.

Slide show: Opening collage shows the twenty-three different abodes in which I spent my childhood—apartments, houses, guesthouses, grandma's living room; urban, rural; a turquoise swimming-pool full of stranger-neighbors here, a two-acre desert ranch there. CLICK. My room. Fundamentals the same in each home. That's me, reading on the bed, aged eight, twelve, seventeen. CLICK. Mom and friends ruddy and laughing on mountain bikes. I'm in the background, crying, face caked with dirt, slapping bugs off my arms, struggling uphill. CLICK. Mom. Moving into a new home, excited by the vast possibility implicit in its newness. CLICK. My partner photographing each row of books in my room, so he can replace them in the correct order once he's finished the built-in shelves that will be my twenty-third birthday present.

Four months after the shelves go up, my mom's planned a trip for the two of us, to Machu Picchu and surrounding areas. Before the flights are confirmed, she gets nervous. Am I really up for this? she asks. Should we be doing something else, heading somewhere full of museums and theaters instead of mountains and muddy trails and backpacks and treacherous roads? I'm fine, I tell her.

Fantasy slide show: Me, strong-legged, clear-headed, and fearless on a path through the clouds. CLICK. Me in a hostel room, writing furiously through the night as my mother sleeps, my acuity sharpened by days of clean air and sense-searing landscapes. CLICK. Finally, me and my mother, talking, open, together, unguarded, fetter-free.

It'll be fine, I tell her again. We're going.

In the weeks between that phone call and departure, I fret over getting a passport at the last minute; whether to get the recommended vaccinations (none are required; my mom opts out on all of them; I finally get the shots at an all-night clinic near the airport, affecting boldness by going without anti-malarial medication); and which books to bring (we'll be backpacking; Mom's instructed me to pack light). I ultimately select Eliot's *Four Quartets* and Lethem's *Motherless Brooklyn,* so I can satisfy the very different reading impulses possible with lightweight paperbacks.

Mom sleeps over the night before our flight. I don't sleep at all, opting to stay up watching early Atom Egoyan films about burnt-down houses and insurance and eerie unfinished tract-home developments and adults in costumed play and suddenly there's the airport shuttle waiting for us. I smile at my mother. I agree it's all very exciting. There is no in-flight conversation because I sleep the whole way.

For the year and a half since, I've been looking for some single image, some entry point, some snapshot more potent, more meaningful than all the others, to do for me the hard work of this sorting, this story-ing. But my head is full of slide shows.

On a path above Machu Picchu, my mother asks me to snap a quick photo of the ruins, being sure to leave the modern, high-priced hotel looming obnoxiously at the park's entrance out of the frame. I ask, knowing exactly, why. But I insist on taking at least one with the hotel in the foreground. I regret my petulance, in that moment like others, but a part of me genuinely dislikes the snapshot. The photos we take in the Andes do nothing to show their immensity, the smallness of us in a valley between them. I find myself snorting at people with cameras held to their faces—my mother, yes, but strangers, too—overwhelmed with disdain at the silly, misguided, even insulting attempts to capture something so large. The snapshot I'm seeking to serve as pithy entrée to this writing is impossible, the desire for it a lazy one. This journey's far too complex to be reduced to a single image.

Alone for a few hours one afternoon, I run up and down the stone steps of Machu Picchu, mind flooded with images, series of film strips speeding fast to their loose-flapping ends, one after another. There's always more than one story.

Mine highlights my mother's decision to transport a large quantity of the liquid extract of an indigenous hallucinogenic plant from one town to another, without determining if it's legal, at the request of a self-identified shaman who leads tours of bourgeois Europeans well-equipped to buy their entrance into new-age enlightenment.

Her version features my general terseness, my disinterest in every activity she suggested, and, finally, my multiple panic attacks, which prompt both her plea that I "stop acting like a two-year-old" and the after-midnight back rubs she gives without complaint to calm my sobbing adult self.

Suddenly, I'm telling it differently, rapturous about the insane grandeur of the Andes, the brilliant sky, my shock at the faded colors of LA after Cuzco's vibrant intensity. But even these tellings lead to the same silent questions: why can't I love it aloud in her presence? What's the impulse to love, appreciate, admire, feel anything, in secret, fiercely protected? There are other questions, of course.

More slides: Us at a table, eating fish and sipping coca tea. Food as distraction, comfort, occupation, pleasure; our days organized around meals; the two of us suddenly united in pursuit of each next one, aimless and somehow empty again once the plates are cleared. CLICK. Me pretending to sleep while she laughs with two Canadian girls, my age, on the train. Next day they'll hike together, all three, while I wait in the hostel room, read a silly mystery I've picked up from the only English bookstore in town. CLICK. The two of us, arms linked, on a cloudy peak, with tired eyes and straining smiles that want so badly to be the recorded face of love and togetherness.

I've long labeled my panic attacks a symptom of culture shock, decided I'm not the traveling kind and left it at that. But the more truthful reason, maybe, is us: my mother and me in close proximity, perpetual contact, yet, somehow, so far apart. Together in form, fact, blood, history, but near silent, awkward and at missteps, estranged.

On the flight to Peru, I had decided, perhaps desperately, that twelve days of clean air, stunning natural beauty, and us-against-nature would sort us all out, force me open and honest, give us, unbarred, to ourselves and each other. On a guilt-ridden, two-days-early, window-staring flight home ten days later, I wondered, earnestly, why I can't ever be satisfied. I didn't consider the impossible height of my expectations.

I think she wanted it, too—a transformation on foreign soil, a cleaning clear and breaking down, knowing each other and walking without tension on a trail lined with wild orchids at 13,000 feet.

But it's harder, this, than a hike at high altitudes, the air thin, at a premium, breath short at the slightest effort. Harder than worrying about theft at every corner, crossing fingers in the back-seat during a stranger's reckless drive in the rain over an endless-seeming series of Andean switchbacks, stammering for help in a half-learned language, ignoring warnings about murdered tourists and unwarranted incarcerations in foreign prisons: harder than all this. This learning and re-learning how to know each other, our-selves, is a trip told again and again, in shifting perspectives. Decades of moments and meanings lie inside each of us, some-times jumping in to support a particular, motivated narrative; sometimes leaping forward unasked, inserting themselves out of order into the slide show of the present.

We keep trying, keep assembling and collecting and framing and re-ordering, envisioning/revisioning, working/reworking, traveling, together, apart, apart, together.

Perhaps Like This Again

by Marjorie Ford

I drive hard, straight west from Hermosillo—the gracious bougainvillea-rich state capital of Sonora, Mexico. My shoulders hunch tightly over the buslike steering wheel of my bile green VW camper, my head pushing forward like a horse striving to cross the finish line. Although I've never been to Bahia Kino on the Sea of Cortés, I am intent on reaching its purportedly peaceful beach town of Kino Nuevo before sunset. I long to see the sun settle into the sea. I don't recall ever having seen such a sight, but it lives somewhere in my mind's eye.

The road is shoulderless, narrow, rutted, and occupied with slow farm trucks missing their taillights. Poverty is the way of life here, clearly, but it's less shocking than it was near the border. There, crossing from Nogales, Arizona, to Nogales, Sonora, my heart sank into the pit of my stomach when I passed children playing near homes made from tin and cardboard, abandoned railroad cars, whatever resourceful parents could manage. My teenage daughter at my side sat silent—stunned or angry, I imagine.

I brought Shelley with me, even though she didn't want to come, because I can't trust her to stay back in Tucson with a friend, neither hers nor mine. Shoplifting. Alcohol. Drugs. Sex. This barely fifteen-year-old sees rules as walls to tear down. Every minute of every day we battle wills, and I'm afraid hers is stronger than mine. Her belligerence unravels and exhausts me as I struggle to keep her safe from the world and the world safe from her—at the same time as I fight to recover from cancer and divorce.

Five hours of quiet, accepting countryside greeted us between Nogales and Hermosillo. We passed small farms without massive machinery, like picture books of bygone days in the United States, and roadside cantinas offering tacos, cerveza, and Coca-Cola. Occasional towns and villages emitted a quality of lively calm, foreign to me. Bright and elaborate handmade shrines to the Virgin of Guadalupe appeared alongside the road. More modest collections of plastic flowers at the bases of painted crosses prayerfully announced deaths along the route.

As time and place unfold, it occurs to me that this trip may be more than a quick escape to the beach, away from Tucson where I try to bury my tension in frenzied activity. By the time we round the curve marking the beginning of the quiet beach town of Kino Nuevo, the sun is long down and darkness hides the bay. A lone truck travels the two-lane street through town. The sidewalk is deserted, except for a few people in front of tiny cantinas. Salsa music wafts from an open window.

"I'm starved!" Shelley demands, her tone more than adolescent high drama.

"We'll eat before we go to sleep," I reply, attempting the tone of a mother to be respected. I drive the length of the town in search of a place to eat. On the beach, just before the road turns to sand and meanders behind the big rock at the end of town, there is an open restaurant. When we enter, we find raucous gringos celebrating Valentine's Day.

The gringos turn out to be North Dakota retirees wintering at the tiny RV park across the street. Several uniformed federales (Mexican federal police that foreign travelers fear), perhaps barely nineteen years old, sit in a corner, quiet and amused.

A salsa band, clearly local, plays, their cowboy hats and shirts stained and worn. One of the three musicians is particularly handsome, with a luscious head of thick black hair and a full mustache, a trim body, and only one leg. I wonder how he keeps his balance. If it's harder to lose a leg or a breast.

Shelley orders a hamburger, fries, and a Coke, and I order steamed clams and a Dos Equis *con limón.* My plate comes piled high, and I share with Shelley, whose meal doesn't measure up to her McDonald's-inspired standards. Before long, a sixty-ish gringa dances on a table, threatening to take off her Valentine's Day T-shirt. She is laughingly booed by the others and comes down from the table, on the edge of becoming an angry drunk, I fear. But the musicians play on, and the mood is accepting. I actually persuade

Shelley to dance with me in the corner. More cautious than I am, even this far from her friends, she is relieved when almost immediately two of the *federales* approach and politely rescue us from each other. They don't flirt, and a sense of safety nudges me toward freedom.

Driving back along the beach, I spot a long open stretch. I pull onto the sand, turn off the engine, pop the camper top, and climb onto the upper bed still clothed. My body sinks easily into the support of the thin mattress.

"Good night, sweetheart," I call down to Shelley.

"Good night, Mom," she calls up to me in a sweet, open voice. I note the change in her tone, and I fall immediately into the rhythm of waves softly washing the edges of my mind.

Just after dawn, I awake to the sensation of a pleading bladder. I pile out of the camper and look up and down a nearly deserted beach. There's nowhere to pee!

Groggy and desperate, I squat in the sand, surprisingly at ease without the burden of my forty-something years of Anglo citification. A local fisherman thirty yards up the beach pays me no attention. He braces himself against his *panga* and steadily mends his fishing net.

The air is light and crisp. Like a sweet elixir, the wet-dry smell of sea and sand awaken my senses, awareness accumulating piece by piece. Beach smells arrive with the distinct and distant flavors of burning mesquite and spicy cooking. The subtle breeze off the water strokes my skin and hair as other winds never have. I welcome the harsh sensation of sand on my feet. A quiet, unimposing magic lays itself before me.

I look up the beach beyond the fisherman to the east end of the bay. Above him a fireball sun reaches a thirty-degree angle. I glance west. The awesome sight of a full moon at the same thirty-degree angle, hanging there on its way into the sea, stops my breath. Here, as if for me to witness, the universe suspends in perfect balance two orbs—one hot, one cool—in complete harmony. A rare, miraculous symmetry. I take a deep breath and hold it full in my lungs, absorbing a sense of wholeness. When the sky changes, that vision of life's perfection nestles into the center of my being where nourishing memories store themselves.

I quietly climb back into the camper as Shelley sleeps soundly. My sneakers are within reach, so I carry them out of the camper and silently close the door. Shelley doesn't like to be disturbed. I have no desire to experience her anger or to watch myself be manipulated by it.

A honey brown-skinned boy, perhaps ten years old, runs along the shore, cheering, toward the water. I look in the direction he is calling and see three black shapes arc in and out of the small swells.

"*¿Qué es eso?*" I yell to him.

"*¡Delfinos negros!*" he yells back.

It seems to be a rare event, dolphins this far into the bay. Or he may just have a ten-year-old's gift for wonder. I remember Shelley's innocent joy at that age.

I run with the dolphins and the boy for awhile, but can't keep up, so I turn and walk back past the camper, toward the huge rock at the far end of the beach. My mind and body recoil, tight again, my feet beating the sand with old ghosts. My thoughts are like a bad country and western song: *How could he leave me for her? Will I ever be loved again?*

Scolding myself for my pain, I barely catch my balance when I slip on the rocks. My body grabs my attention. I relish the sensation of leg muscles tightening to reach for surer footholds, arch and toes grasping through rubber soles toward wet jagged rocks. I climb farther and farther around the huge rock, looking back now and then for a sight of the beach—like a small child, testing herself in the world.

Having rounded the boulder, I no longer see the beach, the town, or my camper. I pass near a man and boy silently fishing with hand-held lines. Then there is no one. I face away from land, toward the sea. The world is vast. I am alone. I like it. I like alone. How can that be?

A familiar panic washes over me like a rogue wave, and I rush back toward the beach. It's already hot, and wind stirs the sand. I sneeze and cough, my eyes watery and red. I stare at the spot where I left Shelley in the camper. They're both gone.

I'd left the camper unlocked with the keys in the ignition.

Shelley must have left . . . or been kidnapped! How could I have left her so vulnerable?

I remind myself that I'm used to her antics—and my reactions to them. It's always the same. First I'm exasperated, assuming she's made trouble. Then I worry that something has happened to her.

She can drive—sort of—I reassure myself. A year ago, I discovered her careening through a shopping center's parking lot, proudly waving to friends congregated in front of a pizza hangout. She wasn't looking straight ahead. She could have wrecked her friend's car. Or worse.

My daughter is still out of control. Like my life.

I rush along the sleepy sidewalk telling myself I should never have relaxed. The entrance to town seems the most likely direction she would have gone—or been taken. Most beach houses are closed up, cantinas not yet open.

A few blocks up the beach near the edge of town, I come upon a small hotel with the camper parked in front. Shelley bounds down the front stairs.

"Where *were* you?!" she scolds like an angry mother.

"I went for a walk while I let you sleep longer. Where were *you*?"

"I woke up and had to go to the bathroom and you were gone!" she accuses. Suddenly her tone turns light. "There's a nice bathroom in the hotel."

"Shelley, you don't have a driver's license," I say, trying to sound firm, but my voice conveys relief that she, the camper, and the town are unharmed.

"Well, you weren't there, Mom!" she declares. Then swiftly, "Can we have breakfast here? I'm starved."

It's her customary approach: A good offense as defense followed by a light distraction. It works today as it usually does. Even when I'm aware of her tactics I am helpless to counter them. She is skilled at getting what she wants, a quality I've wanted for my daughter since before she was born.

I want to linger over my breakfast of huevos rancheros and rich coffee. Shelley is surprisingly content with this slower pace. We spend the morning unaware of time, eating and looking out the big picture window at the bay across the street, talking easily about nothing in particular. I tell her how I saw the rising sun and setting moon hanging in perfect balance. And I tell her of the awe and wholeness I felt. She actually seems interested, pleased for me. We haven't been this connected since David left. Or maybe we have been—by pain and fear.

As we leave the hotel restaurant, I stop to admire the ironwood carvings of a Seri Indian boy from the nearby village.

"*¿Haces tú estes?*" I ask cautiously in my high-school Spanish.

"*No, los hicieron mi mamá y papá.*"

His black eyes shine with pride.

I pick up three dolphins and stroke the ironwood; its silky texture and rich dark tones are exquisite.

"You want them, Mom, get them," Shelley prods, encouraging my pleasure. She's right. I want all three of these fine creatures. The artisans have captured their joyful motion, at once light and solid. Their life connected to itself and all around them. Like the dolphins who frolicked in the bay this morning. Like this place. Like me here.

When Shelley and I climb into the camper, I wrap the carvings in a T-shirt and prepare for the trip home. On the long drive back to Tucson, we are easy with each other. We share comfortable silences, laughter, and reactions to the serene simplicity of the countryside and the jarring poverty at the border.

I remember us like this. Before life fell apart. Before I fell apart. I remember. Perhaps it will be like this again.

Minding the Gap

by Mary Morris

We were sitting at the dining room table when the thought came to me. I was trying to get my eleven-year old daughter to talk about her day and eat her meal; she sat with her legs tucked under her, offering what had become her usual monosyllabic responses to our questions. If my husband, Larry, and I let her, she'd have dinner with her headset on.

This was not the child I knew. My daughter used to bubble with excitement, sharing each tidbit of her day, each goofball cafeteria anecdote. But lately she seemed almost indifferent to me. She and I used to share everything—hot baths, long reading sessions in bed, walks to school. Now we read in separate rooms, if she reads at all. She walks to school with her pals.

A friend of ours whose children were all in high school had warned me. "When they turn thirteen, they're gone." Kate, our only child, was on the brink of adolescence, and I was starting to feel that the mothering part of my life was done. Where had those years gone? Our time at home was parceled out between phone calls and email. I had been extremely busy with my career as a writer and teacher, and Kate had school and a demanding basketball and volleyball schedule.

Though she sat across from me, I found myself missing my own daughter. That was when I turned to her and said, "How about just you and me taking a vacation over spring break?"

She peered up from the food that was circling her plate. Her tired brown eyes widened. We had always traveled well together and I saw I'd lit a spark. "Sure," she said, "where?"

I mulled it over in my mind. London would be nice, but too civilized. A spa? Too easy. The Andes. Too rough. Then I recalled the seaside trip we'd all loved in Montego Bay when she was six.

"Let's go to the Caribbean. We can go snorkeling."

Her dad, a journalist, was all for it. "It would be great if you girls had some time together that was all yours," he agreed.

It was late to get reservations for spring break, but the Holiday Inn at Grand Cayman had a room available for five nights. Planning the trip gave us something to do together. We bought guidebooks to coral fish, to shells and coral. Kate had always been a nature lover, and I felt this trip would rekindle her interest as well as our interest in each other.

In the weeks before our journey we made a pact. We would bring no electronic devices: no Discman or Gameboy for Kate, no laptop for me. We would have books, journals, and our own adventures. But on the plane Kate wanted to play hangman all the way to Grand Cayman. After an hour or so I was ready to pull out a novel.

"Why don't we read or relax?" I suggested.

"If you'd let me bring my Discman," she complained.

On arrival, Kate was reluctant to help carry the luggage. She said the bags were too heavy; I told her to "pitch in." I had thrown my back out ice-skating and couldn't believe I hadn't brought suitcases on wheels. We were tired, but our hotel was in worse shape.

Despite being nicely situated on the beach, it was slated for demolition the following week. Morale was low, services were poor. Our room had an air conditioner that clanged like a train engine and no view of the sea which disappointed us both. "Let's see if we can't get a nicer room," I said. Kate flopped on the bed.

I got us a room right on the beach, but I thought, how often do I take a trip like this with my daughter?

As we moved the luggage again, we were barely speaking. Kate loved the new room, however, and soon began to relax. Once we were settled, we headed for the sand where we saw someone parasailing high above the waves.

"Hey, Mom," Kate said, "I want to do that."

I thought about my aching back. "Well, you can go alone," I told her, "That's not my cup of tea."

Already we seemed to be falling into our old patterns. I'd imagined that this vacation would somehow make the barriers and obstacles melt away, but it was obvious that it hadn't. I wanted my books and solace. Kate wanted to play in the pool and stay up late, listening to the Barefoot Man, the house band. I was up at six, ready to explore; she slept until ten. I spent my early mornings longing for my computer, walking a lonely beach. Once Kate woke up, she was grumpy and it wasn't until noon that the day could begin.

I knew in my maternal gut that we had to strike a balance. On one of my solitary mornings I had discovered the hotel's daily snorkeling adventures to Stingray City and signed us up. The boat left at 10 A.M., which meant Kate had to be up at nine. She was tired, but soon there were baby stingrays, resting in her hands, swimming through our legs. We visited the cavern of a spotted moray eel (named Mama) and stroked the back of a nurse shark.

That night we slept soundly. And the next morning we eagerly went on another excursion, to the wreck of the Cali, where Kate found the hiding place of a giant sea turtle and swam with it as if out to sea. We developed a language for being underwater together—we would point and give a thumbs-up if something was great, and make a time-out signal if we were ready for a break.

A fellow traveler had told us that Cemetery Reef was an easy place to snorkel alone, that lots of people went there and that despite its ominous name, it was safe. Kate liked the idea of going out on our own, so the next day I bought lunch at a nearby market and we hopped in a cab. We found ourselves on an almost deserted strip of pure white sand ringed by coconut palms. We placidly kicked in the warm waters until we came upon a huge orange and purple reef and we swam across the top of it, pointing out the fish we wanted each other to see. Kate seemed happy when the school of palm-sized black and yellow fish approached us. Soon, they surrounded her, and before I knew what was happening, they began to nip at her. She flailed, fighting them off.

As she reached for me I saw that she was terrified, and I swam her to shore. When she got out, she ripped off her mask. She was trembling, on the verge of tears.

"I'm not going back," she said, "I'm not going in that water again."

I understood her fear, but I was trying to understand why the fish had attacked her and left me alone. As I was comforting her, I felt the gold chain around her neck.

"Honey, it's the chain."

I knew this much about being in water: you aren't supposed to swim with shiny objects on your body; the fish think it's a smaller fish. "Here, let's take it off."

Still she refused. My daughter's stubborn side and her vulnerable side can become one and the same, but I know the importance of getting back on the horse when you've fallen off.

"I promise you," I told her, "if they bother you again, we'll get right out of the water and you'll never have to get back in."

I took her chain and stashed it in the dive bag. Then we put on our flippers and masks. As we were stepping into the water,

Kate reached for me. "Mommy," she said, "hold my hand." We swam together to the reefs, hand in hand, and the fish did not bother her again.

Back at the hotel, the Barefoot Man Band played at a seafood buffet. We ate, danced, and headed to bed before ten. En route to our room, we paused before a man who inscribes your name on a grain of rice. Kate had him write hers, then seal it in a dolphin-shaped charm.

That night, my daughter who was poised on the brink of adolescence, my girl who was almost "gone," called out to me half asleep.

"Mommy," she said, "hold my hand."

And I reached across the pillow and held it the whole night long.

The next day she was up early. When she asked what we were doing, I said we were going parasailing. I trembled as two men strapped me into the harness and plunked Kate between my legs. I wrapped my arms around her and, as we rose above the sea, started to scream. I screamed and screamed, absolutely terrified, my back hurting, and felt Kate clutch my hands.

"It's all right, Mommy," she said. "Look, it's beautiful."

And as we sailed in the air up and down the shore, past palm trees, my daughter clasped to me, it really was.

Our getaways are becoming a regular thing. Right now we're thinking about a friend's invitation to Hawaii, or a hike on the Inca Trail. But it doesn't always have to be a big trip. It might just be what we call spa day, when we take hot baths and slather ourselves with mud. Or an afternoon of shopping and lunch in Chinatown. What matters is this: I've learned to recognize when Kate's asking for my help and when she wants to be on her own. And she has learned that she can grow up and still ask me to hold her hand.

Release

Cashing Out on the Bering Sea

by Martha Sutro

I'm sorting crab and can't keep up. I grab a shell, yank its legs from a tangled mass, and toss it into a tank. A ton of unsorted monsters, like a heap of slag, clicks and sloshes around me. I can't keep up. Dislodged crabs, unsorted, back away by the dozens across a shining deck. Another hand, another crab: I yank it, toss it. Waist-high in sea muck and tangled lines, I'm stuck in a sewing machine that won't turn off. Crabs and shells, octopi and lost fish surge up my legs. Codfish and halibut too big to handle rip and flap from the slag. A film of seawater trickles into my breath. The halibut slips from my gloves. A hard wave slaps the back of my hood. Ocean water drips from its brim, stings my eyes. Seawater fills my breath. I can't sort fast enough, can't wipe the sting off, can't hold on.

If you were a mother, this might concern you: your daughter slipping between anonymous waves, out of the reach of any reliable signal short of a Coast Guard contact, on a sea so distant the planet nearly renders it polar. She's working on a hundred-foot boat with five men you've never known and wouldn't want to, in an industry that *Forbes* ranks second only to coal mining in danger, as ranked by number of work-related deaths per year. My mother rips the article from the pages of the magazine and tapes it to the refrigerator in her Virginia kitchen.

Obsession is the boat's name. The captain, Ted Goss. I met him two years ago when we'd both signed on to a climbing trip in the Alaska Range. Leaving Alaska at the end of that trip, Ted said to me, "If you ever want to crab-fish on the Bering Sea, give me a call," as if offering a weekend holiday.

In the intervening two years I saw Ted twice, once on the West Coast, once on the East. His life was determined by plane schedules, fishing openings, and the weather. I taught at a tiny school in northern Vermont, and when he visited for a weekend one spring he brought a pile of newspapers—*The Kodiak Daily Mirror*—and a cooler full of crab. His letters read like lists. Sometimes he sent just lists—of gear, catch quotas, and location readings off his boat's Loran system. I absorbed every scrap of evidence received from his world.

Obsessed with a vision of a faraway life at the hand of a transient, foreign figure, I defended my connection to Ted unequivocally to my mother, even though I did not define my relationship to him in my own mind. We flirted over the phone, bought a couple of weekend plane tickets that flung us together enough to let us know we wanted a longer experience. We avoided talk that would define us, and focused instead on defining an arrangement that would suit us both. At the same time, we kept that arrangement comfortably unclear, making no promises, signing no contract, setting no end point. All I needed to do was show up in Dutch Harbor at the beginning of February, ready to work.

A month before I left for Alaska, I received a package from Ted. Inside, I found only texts: a worn copy of a book dramatically titled *Working on the Edge,* its cover photos a wash of orange bodies blurred against a veil of green water. There were also a few random nautical charts: *Shumagin Island to Sarak Islands, Alaska Peninsula and Aleutian Islands to Seguam Pass,* and one unmarked video.

That night I sat on my living-room floor and stuck the video into the TV set. The image on the screen floated steadily out to reveal a nebulous, pancaked mass, an ice pack. White and white and white against a terminally gray sky, against slivers of a shaley sea, rising slowly, sinking slowly. The frame panned from the stern-mounted wheelhouse of the vessel, where the camera was filming, up towards the bow of the boat, showing the deck in between, a low, rectangular space enclosed like the sunken stage of a theater. Ice shagged the boat's railings. Rusty pots, hoses, boxes, coils of line, equipment I couldn't recognize sat usefully but quietly in the frame, like farm equipment looks when it rests, dirt-encased, in between shifts.

The shot drifted back to the sea. A disembodied voice outside the frame of the picture made a simple, muffled comment: "Pretty tight pack." Nobody answered. There was just the static of a nylon sleeve in the wind, and the sound of wind shifting and rising. *Not a lot of speech in this world,* I thought, *but a thousand kinds of cold.* No work, either, when the hull of the boat is hugged by a shoreless game board of packed ice. The coarse wind sound surged from the television set, died, resurged. The image on the screen floated back to the deck, up to the bow. Boat to sea. Sea to boat. That's all there was.

I was sitting cross-legged on the carpet. My mother watched silently behind me in a chair, waiting for something imminent onscreen. When nothing happened, I turned the set off, saying, "Hmm. Great ice."

No response. I tried again.

"Looks pretty chilly."

She didn't acknowledge either idea, only waited a minute and asked, as if to herself, "Why in the world would you want to go to a place like that?"

I paused, allowing the question to ring with a dramatic hollowness. The grandfather clock in the hall struck and rested. Outside, a mild winter breeze pushed rain across the sycamore trunks and I thought of the lacy fingers of ice on the stanchions of the *Obsession.*

"Because I want to see the Bering Sea in winter," I stated, with a pilgrim's importance.

I had no real answer for her. All I knew was that I needed to be saved from the directness of that question.

On a late January day I stood at the Richmond airport, a wool sweater itching my neck, my duffel of sweatshirts, socks, and mittens packed and already on the airplane. My mother stood in front of me as a dim sense of ambivalence I'd had for a week sharpened into a crisp panic.

"I'm certain I should, of course, absolutely and without hesitation, cancel this plan," I heard myself say.

Not five months earlier Mother was putting me on a plane for Kathmandu, the starting point for my solo journey through the Himalayas. "See you in three months," I said at that departure, acting out a carefree persona she could see right through. In between trips into the Nepalese mountains, I'd called home every day, sometimes twice. I knew Mom could see straight into this paradox: intrepid as I looked in my own eyes, what she often heard was a string of hesitations mixed in amidst bold declarations. From Kathmandu's telephones, those litanies cost a dollar a minute.

On that January day in the Richmond airport, Mom stood in flats and a green overcoat, a dutiful confidence written into her eyes. She looked me over, top to bottom, wishing she'd polished the hiking boots I was wearing. I was twenty-seven, but she was thinking about what a child needs when she packs for summer camp—if only it were summer camp that winter day. I paused a minute, to see if she could detect the rising, internal vertigo in me. The passengers were gone, the desk attendant called for the stragglers. Mom hugged me hard around the neck, saying "Call us when you get there."

Her shoulders pressed against mine and a quick, fortuitous signal reached me with an unreal intensity. *I'm meant to stay here in the soft southern winter,* I thought, *perhaps get a job at a sandwich shop.* I spoke.

"Ma, maybe I'll stay. Maybe this is a dumb idea. Maybe I should just not go."

She hugged me again, not so tight this time, neither caught off guard nor willing to accept my hesitation.

"You've gotten yourself into this," she said. "You've got to see where it's taking you."

Amazed and speechless, I turned from her, my panic converting to astonishment. I walked down the long throat of the airplane entryway, her eyes following me the entire way.

I imagine water, and the ways of water. Water, like a torrent of verb forms, becomes the atmosphere of my imagination. Flying across the continent, past its edge and out towards its hooked and fragile tip, I realize that I have known Ted in person for the sum total of only twenty days. Capricious, elastic, familiar, dreams of seas sink and surge in my mind. The saltiest water I've known is the Chesapeake's, an almost deciduous sort of liquid, soft and safe, resilient. As a child, I'd head out on the bay in Sailfish boats alone, or with my brother when the wind picked up. We mastered the ways of submerging. Pull and pull on the mainsheet. Stay close to the wind. Watch the mast tip into view, then downward to the surface, closer, until momentum slacks and slacks some more. A little sea foam. The sail meeting the wave. A jump, an easy fall backwards over the hull. The miniature bravery of the capsize. Grab the centerboard, kick once with your legs, climb on in time with the boat righting, the boom shuddering nervously, the bright sail dripping in the sun.

Fog and clouds matte the iron-streaked Gulf of Alaska and the Bering Sea all winter—indeed, for most of the year. On a plane, looking down, nothing appears, nothing, until a grind of wheels dislodges from the plane's belly. Suddenly, barren islands—the lonely hummocks of the Aleutians—rise white and wind-scoured; there is not a single tree. A Russian Orthodox church, its tips as brown against snow as burnt onions, casts the gloom of a forgotten country on the margin of a bay. This is Dutch Harbor.

From above, container ships, crab boats, freighters, draggers, a tugboat all appeared as toys. Pickup trucks, vans, and supply trucks routed through potholed, muddy roads. At this first sight, the clouds slung low, the ocean swelling, tracked by chords of foam, I let my head fall back against the seat rest and only looked down from the corner of my eye. A loose knot shifted in my stomach. I had never been on a winter sea.

The second day there I found a pay phone in the entryway to Stormy's pizza place in Unalaska, the village across the island from Dutch Harbor. Through the static of the distance, the phone rang in Virginia.

"This place feels like the end of the earth," I told my mother, delighted that I had made it that far, and feeling that my successful arrival boded well for my career in crab fishing.

She responded with a weak, "Oh," wishing she could say nothing at all.

Did I need her approval? Did I need to show her that I didn't need her approval, in spite of what I needed? She had already begun a kind of endurance test—a daily, weekly terror-management seminar, forcing excruciating detachment, unable to restrain her intense bewilderment or her engagement with the highlights of my choice to go this far.

Outside the cracked glass of the phone booth the wind ramped in off the harbor. A rusty pickup, its bed loaded with coils of line, splashed through snowflakes blowing sideways. Someone else was waiting for the phone. I finished raving about the glory of that remoteness, hung up, zipped up my jacket, and took off across driveways and dirt parking lots, making my way down to a black beach rimmed by clapboard houses, junked cars, and totem poles. Every so often, a big wintry dog looked my way through eyes covered in blown fur.

I got my fishing gear at Carl's General Store, in the middle of town. I got a blue wool cap, a pair of brown steel-toed fishing boots, orange bibbed overalls, and an orange hooded slicker, made by a Norwegian company called Grundens. I got several pairs of rubber fishing gloves and polypropylene liner gloves to go inside them. My biggest investment was a Stormy Seas jacket that I would wear all the time, even under the slicker. It was warm, lined in pile, and fitted with a deflated cushion for flotation. Inside the left chest pocket was a CO_2 cartridge and a ripcord.

"If you end up in the water out there," Ted had said to me as I set off for Carl's with a list of gear he had written for me, "that jacket will help you stay afloat until we can come around and get you."

I was the only new member of the crew this season, and I went alone, with Ted's suggestions, to buy the gear. I spent $300 and walked back to the boat, carrying my goods in a plastic shopping bag.

Tanks full of gas and water, cupboards stocked with food, the bait freezer full, and the deck loaded with 60 pots ready for fishing, we drove out of Dutch the next morning at 3:00 A.M., motoring past other draggers and fishers silently clustered in packs and lit by sodium lights on their rigging. Ahead of us, Priest Rock marked the entrance to the harbor. The sea, further out, was as black and still as ink in a well.

How is it I had come to that moment, driving out to the middle of the Bering Sea with five men I barely even knew? Ted had introduced me to the men on the crew with a simple, "Martha will be fishing with us." Bob, an old-time fisherman, accepted me immediately with a kind of sad friendliness. All in their twenties like me, Bill, Steve, and Mike made up the rest of the crew. They formed a kind of brotherhood, sharing a stateroom, a lingo, and a quiet admiration for Ted. I knew they were waiting to test me on deck. They were in no hurry to accept an East Coast English teacher who had never even been on a fishing boat.

After two days of driving, we reached the fishing grounds, a region of water that looked, on the surface, no different than any other stretch of ocean. The bow of the *Obsession* was charging through a flinty chop. Spray, caught by a 35-knot wind, slapped on the rigging. The crab pots we carried, stacked 3-deep, rose like an enormous square cake, its utmost height 40 feet from the ocean waves.

The Bering Sea extends a lonely and storm-fraught 1,600 miles westward from the coast of Alaska to Russia; for the first 400 of those westward pushing miles, the continental shelf forms its floor and is home to the greatest stores of king crab on the planet. The water, rarely more than 600 feet deep on the shelf, makes crab fishing relatively manageable. It is the Bering Sea weather—moody, monotonous, sometimes monstrous—that fishermen must endure in order to harvest the crab.

To each of the crab pots on our deck we've tied together and then attached three separate coils of line, called shots. At rest on the sea floor, each line will string to a pair of buoys, called a setup, that floats on the surface. Eight to fifteen pots, set in the space of a nautical mile or two and resting on the ocean floor, form a string. The skipper sets his strings of pots where he's historically found or hopes to find crab. As we set the pots overboard, Ted, who drives the boat from his control post up in the wheelhouse, enters the location of each pot and its string into a computer called a plotter. Miraculously, we could spend two days crossing a seascape as undefined as a frozen desert, and arrive exactly where we left a string of buoy setups, tugging and bobbing on the misty sea, several days before.

On my first day of deck work, I pulled my boots on over thick socks, and my orange Grundens bibs over long underwear, sweatpants, and the Stormy Seas jacket. The wind-ripped rollers ahead of the Obsession bore thick crests of foam that broke across the bow and the side rigging. Out the windows of the wheelhouse, I noticed the crab pots on deck were coated in a thick, frozen spray. It was morning. We were going to bait the pots we had on deck and set them in this stretch of ocean. Bob and the rest of the boys, well-sealed in their own Grundens, clamored around me and made their way out the side doors of the wheelhouse, and then across the crab pots stacked on deck. I could not get the straps of my bibs adjusted, so Ted tied them with a string in back, saying calmly, "Don't worry, you'll be fine out there. Just listen to Bob and you'll be fine."

I snapped up my jacket, promising myself I wouldn't be late or last or even slow.

Once the wheelhouse door shut behind me, my first objective was clear: get up to the bow of the boat where the boys stood, somewhat protected, between the stacked pots on deck and the forepeak, a tiny room wedged into the bow section of the vessel. Getting to this island of safety would involve a couple of tricks, tricks I'd mastered easily when the boat was in Dutch, when the pots on deck seemed like nothing more demanding than an extravagant jungle gym. Out on the open sea, the jungle gym lurched hysterically and unpredictably. To get from the wheelhouse to my first step on the pots, I swung my body out over the water, my feet on the rail of the boat, and saw, between the toes of my new brown boots, our churning wake 30 feet below. Human beings don't last ten minutes in that water, even if they're floating in Stormy Seas jackets.

I stepped up onto the stack of pots and stood on their bars as if they were railroad ties. I stretched out my arms and moved slowly and evenly. No falls, no crawling on my ass—I made it all the way across them and up to the forepeak. I had no idea what I was supposed to do when I got there, except follow the orange shapes ahead. I did know that I was afraid of two things: not being strong enough to do the work, and not knowing a single thing about what I was doing.

Nouns present potential: gravity, buoyancy, sand, sun, crab, objects in space with no stake in movement or time. A boat on a blank sea. A crab pot tipped swiftly off the boat and still visible, just for a moment, before coils of speed and space take it, a red buoy its only suggestion. Nouns, so many, become the matters of importance on a fishing boat. How many pots? How many strings of pots? How many feet in these particular shots in this particular string? How many knots, as in knots on the pot ties, and how many knots, as in boat speed, as in wind speed? How many nautical miles? How many gallons of gas? How cold? How fast? How high? How many? Nouns are clay, potential, energy, waiting for the integrity of some movement.

My first day of work I spent at a kneel. Under the shelter deck, a kind of porch roof covering a forward corner of the deck, the metal bait box, bolted to the rolling deck, was a place I could work with in only one way, by kneeling, set back on my heels so I could use my lap. The red-lidded jars with holes in them were just small enough to fit in my rubber-gloved hand, but not nearly tacky enough. I jammed them against the side of the bait box, against my slippery thighs, between my knees and the box, anything to hold them while I stuffed bits of herring in them, screwed on the lid and then attached the jar onto a wire hook.

I plugged the bait jars as full as possible with the slimy fish bits. When the bait box emptied, I rose, gray and pink flecks of herring covering my front sides, herring somehow stuck in my hair, and tipped unsteadily across a bucking deck for several feet to the bait freezer. I dislodged a 50-pound box of frozen herring, opened and thrust the icy chunk into a chopper where a blade, operating with a deafening clatter, made a silvery, icy mush ready for the bait jars.

* * *

The proverbial shelter deck was the salon of this dignified process. The sound of wind in my ears, a sound I would come to recognize permanently, one doesn't find shelter from anywhere, ever, on the boat. At my kneel for long stretches of work, I shifted between weather systems: the one on the empty slate horizon, which I watched continually as if expecting an appearance; the one on deck, where four men I hardly knew kept at their tasks with pots and lines and crabs; and the one in my stomach, a cemented, granular grind.

My first day, second day, third, my first night, my whole first fishing trip, two weeks long, was not about work, it was about surviving. It was about negotiating mistakes, learning how to step forward or back on a steep deck, how to stand and work out of the wind's direct blasts, how to stay out of the way of the work that was not mine.

Steve and the boys had each other to keep up with, and one of the ways they did that was to each yell at me as much as they could. I didn't have this job from walking the docks of Kodiak or Dutch Harbor like they did, I had it from a connection, from luck. I'd ended up with the privileged option of adventure, not the requirement of it. Mixing a little resentment for me with a bit of curiosity, they kept me at a distance. I heard in Dutch Harbor that some skippers believe that that it's never a good idea to have a woman on board a fishing boat, especially a crabber. Ted doesn't think that, but I already knew that it was tricky to sleep with the guy who was driving the boat and work on deck with the guys who weren't.

I was what they call a half-share in the fishing wage world, and Steve, full share like everyone else, was the fiery deck boss. My knowledge that I should never correct a single word of his speech was my only sustaining intelligence on deck. Silence was not a comfortable state for me, but I moved, kneeled, stuffed, stood, and obeyed, mostly in perfect silence. Steve narrated: his impressions of the weight of each incoming pot or the wind; his guess at how long we would work that shift. He would tell me to speed the hell up on the bait, and yell hard and quick at me whenever I came within ten feet of a launching pot or the lines and buoys spewing overboard after it: "Stay the fuck away from the fuckin' lines!"

I could do this. Fuckin' wind. Fuckin' crab. Fuckin' pot. Fuckin' deck boss.

Steve compared crabs, whenever possible, to humans in a vigorous, elaborate sex act. When the pot surfaced, its webbing strained by the load, Steve calibrated the degree of heat in the bait "like hung-a-ry men on the hott-est pussy." The wave hitting over our heads was frigid. Mixed with snow, it was enough to kill any of us if we weren't in rubber outfits, and even if we were. Steve said he wanted some warm pussy. Warm pussy would make that frigid, stunned feeling disappear. Bill, who sat heavily on a stool and ran the hydraulic crane, contended, dangerously in my opinion, that Steve hadn't ever really felt that much warm pussy.

Steve shot back, "You fuck, you've never ever had any piece of pussy. "

I wanted to edit, say "particle of pussy" maybe, but the wind was surging, my voice was too deep in my hood, and by the tenets of the crab-fishing world, Steve, hard-working, tough, and top brother on that deck, really had nothing to lose, even if every claim and narration he made felt like a provocation directed specifically at me.

When we weren't working, we were eating or sleeping. Upstairs in the wheelhouse, Ted stayed in his stateroom bunk, even when the big swells were running. The high swells made me green, and on those stormy nights I slept down below where the roll wasn't so wild. On really rough nights, when I stumbled out of my bunkroom and out into the florescent light of the galley, I sometimes saw Ted sleeping down below too, stretched out in a sweatshirt and jeans on a bench at the galley table.

Buried down in a pit of the boat, only a few feet and a few panels from the boat's engine, my bunk was the only zone of privacy I had for several thousand miles around. Letters, crumpled editions of *The Kodiak Daily Mirror,* yesterday's socks, a ratty sleeping bag, and a sole clean sweatshirt were all stuffed along the edges. It was a room, a bed, and a refuge all at once. I slept on top of my hardcover copy of *To the Lighthouse* and I didn't even know it.

Bob had the bunk above me. Bob Boyle. He was the oldest guy on board, the gentlest, most self-effacing, most enduring member of the crew. He'd been working off and on for Ted for twenty years. Forlorn, accepted, he drank so much whenever the boat was in town that he pickled his withered body. He chain-smoked through his days, slept so soundly he seemed barely alive. I never knew, when I gasped awake from nightmares of crab crawling through my sleeping bag, whether Bob was up in the wheelhouse on watch or just right up above me in the bunk, sound asleep. He had a wife in Anchorage, and only sometimes saw the two children whose school photos were tacked above his bunk. He fished to keep them going. Bones and skin, faded fishing shirts, the same black jeans, he slipped in and out of the stateroom like a weary old cat for smokes behind the windbreak just outside the wheelhouse.

I pictured my mother leaning against the dishwasher in her kitchen, a late February sun breaking across boxwood bushes out the window, the *Forbes* article straight ahead in her gaze, the notes of a Chopin etude filtering through from the living room.

We were on a quick run back to town to resupply and return to the fishing grounds, and I was at a phone booth at the fuel dock in Unalaska. We'd delivered 8,500 pounds of crab from a ten-day trip at $1.92 a pound, and we were due to leave town in an hour. How cold was it? How hard was the work? What clothes do I wear? I avoided telling her about the inflatable Stormy Seas jacket, and avoided answering questions in detail. The vagueness in my answers was a replica of the distance I'd started to feel from her.

Drawn, if not to the point of obsession, then perhaps to the point of compulsion, to Ted's unconventional, hard-working, dangerous, distant life, I'd been following resolutely behind him. I'd learned to scramble to dress for work when we were nearing the gear. Bob and I traded off on the cooking chores, and I knew when to wrap up my tasks on deck and head into the galley to scramble eggs as the end of our shift grew closer. I staggered from my bunk to the wheelhouse for my watch duty when Bob or Ted came to wake me, and when our tanks were full and we were heading for a delivery, I learned how to radio the cannery with our information. I had fallen into a partnership of work and companionship with Ted that felt remote from my first unsure journey across the pots and distant from my other lives and the movements of other people I'd known.

One February night we were working on deck. I was bent over, shoving crab into the hole to the holding tanks below deck, when a wave cleared the railing and hit me full against my backside with the force of a frozen concrete wall. I went down on one knee. My other leg stepped in the manhole-sized tank opening. Suddenly I was flat on my stomach on deck, leg in icy water up to my hip, as off-balance and unsteady as I'd been when I stepped in a crevasse on a glacier. Water filled my boot. I could feel the touch of crab shells through rubber. I didn't say *Shit.* I didn't say *Fuckin' shit.* I coughed for air. The wave left the deck awash, its own small sea. Thirty feet above us, even the windows of the wheelhouse were dripping. I didn't know exactly what had happened, but I felt a flash of terror, of aggressive peril, something I hadn't known in weeks, just submerging one limb in the icy tank. I pulled my leg out, my sock dense with freezing seawater, and ran back to the shelter deck, hoping the boys hadn't seen me fall. I was shaking with fear. The skin on my hip felt raw and moist against my sweats. No one said anything. A few minutes later, I heard Ted's voice on the microphone he used to communicate with us on deck. "I can't see shit out here and I'm lost. Let's finish up in the morning."

Once inside, the boys went down below to the galley to mow through hot dogs, pizza, and Mountain Dew. I sat up in the dark pilot room, looking out at the glistening, empty deck, pulling salt and scraps of herring out of my hair, and rubbing my swollen hands. In front of me the instrument lights glowed orange and green. Ted silently, methodically reset the electronic plotter, changed our course, and pulled the weather map off the fax machine. I knew he saw that wave.

"You don't have to stay out here, fishing, you know," he said.

The fax machine ticked and slowly disgorged another map. Since our weather moved towards us across the Pacific from Japan, I'd imagined that the faxed weather maps did, too. I sometimes imagined that we were actually near Japan. When I looked up sometimes on deck, the red sun broke the somber cloud cover, and slipped silently below the horizon, right into Asia. I didn't say anything to Ted.

"There are much better jobs out there than this one, I know that," he said, pressing me.

The sudden, fricative, disabling slap of a wave from behind is a permanent form, stuck in its sharpness like a car impact, like the clap of wooden boom against skull bone. I said nothing.

Lies, lies, lies. I'd told my mother enough to comprise an entire parallel life, a fiction as intricate as a pile of webbed crab legs. Lies seemed part of the fabric of our knowing each other, related and unrelated at once as we could seem. Mother wrote me long letters, front and back, that I picked up at the cannery in Dutch when we made it to town. She insisted on close presence, she insisted on contact. I had little to offer her in return.

If I could have justified crab fishing to myself, I'd have justified it to her. How could I validate something that seemed, at bottom, about simply asking a set of questions about myself? I thought at the time that my attachment to Ted was my tie to fishing, but, looking back, that wasn't what was keeping me at sea. The cost of the freedom of crabbing is too high for many people. For me, the ultimate liberty of the enterprise seemed to be the drawing card, but it was actually investigating the cost that was the real lure. I didn't know and I couldn't know what that cost was, how far I was willing to go into a self I had never before known. I didn't know how much I could cash out, and that overwhelming unknown was more compelling to me than the freedom, the love affair, the stories, the money in my half-share pocket.

Selfishly, I sent Mom postcards. Selfishly, I told her the crabbing was excellent, that we never worked at night, that Ted and I were great working friends, and that was it. The men were protective and kind. The Alaskan weather had been unusually mild. I had almost made enough money to justify the worry. I would be home in the summer to look for real work in a real place.

We were baiting this pot and throwing it right back over. I left Bob to finish sorting crab at the sorting table, turned, raced to grab a bait set-up, and jogged back to the launch. We were in, maybe, 30-foot swells, but by then, at the end of February, it wasn't difficult to handle big swells anymore. I was doing several jobs on deck at once. Mike hauled shots of line out of the coiler and tossed a couple of them on top of the pot that sat hip-high on the launch. It was my job to bait the pot: with the door open, I sat backwards into the pot. Leaning back, balanced by one hand grasping the top iron bar of the door frame, my other arm reached with the dangling bait setup that would snap to the middle of the pot. No pausing here. My feet stuck out the front of the pot and came up off the deck as my torso, arms, and head extended and tilted back. For a second, I was deep in the pot. I saw all the sky and sea between the diamonds of webbing. Mike and Steve were coiling lines, Bob was stuffing bait jars. I was sitting in the most precarious spot onboard, inside a crab pot that was moments from tipping seaward.

The dangers were these: one, if Bill hit the launch switch, the bars that the pot sits on would lift my legs further from the deck and I would slip, headfirst, upside down, into the passing waves like a ballerina in a music box. Two, if I thought about this, I wouldn't be able to keep up. My stomach aching from the reach, I snapped the bait string in place in a mere second, and swung forward, my head low to clear the upper bar of the pot and then out. Bob and I pulled the door over and down with a yank, stretched and fastened the rubber door ties, and stepped back. Steve hit the switch.

Of all the distinctive sounds from the crab-fishing world—the whine of the coiler, the hiss of the hydraulic block, the crunch of crab refuse between rubber boot soles and deck boards—there is no more impressive sound than that of a crab pot falling into the sea. A crash and a seethe all at once, a mass of foam, a percolation, water gathering in it.

A run into Dutch, in the middle of my second season, and I dashed to the cannery to check for the boat's mail and messages. In the pile was a pink note for me, instructing me to call home as soon as I could. When I did, I was impatient, feeling more possessively sealed into the fishing world than ever. I was competent, accepted. I was more of Ted's equal and less of his project.

Mom answered the phone in Virginia and quickly, excitedly, got down to business. Someone from an office in Denver had called her looking for me, and they wanted me to fill in on a crew that was leaving to work in Antarctica in a month. I was shocked, and I worked to remember that I had eagerly applied for the job—

driving forklifts as part of a cargo crew at the South Pole station—over two years before.

"You'll consider it, won't you?" Mom was trying to be diplomatic here, trying not to plead, but I could hear a pull in her voice.

One tether bound me tautly to Ted and the boat, one tether bound me to her. When did one of them snap from the strain? When did Antarctica become a better option for a daughter? Through the window of the cannery office I saw the mountains of Dutch smudged and muddy, the *Obsession* motoring wearily across the harbor towards the fuel dock, snow ripping sideways in a squall between me and it.

"Yeah, okay, Ma. I'll call the guy. I promise," I said

I had to run to meet the boys, but as I did, I already saw them differently, as if my perception of them were beyond my control. Were they dirtier? Less united? Less hopeful? I had tried to commit my every cell to them, and now I felt like a traitor, something they had suspected me of being all along, someone with a few too many options.

Towards the end of that trip, we worked almost incessantly against the closing date of crab season. It was night when we started working, or else we had been working and I had missed night falling. A night like any other, our orange raingear blurred against the crab and equipment, a team of rugged, forgotten actors on a remote and perilous stage. Snowflakes flung down across the deck, the pots, the rim of the bait box. I couldn't see anywhere,

anywhere outside the sodium lights, couldn't make out even a single feature of night. It was like I was in space. I saw the wheelhouse, its windows black, knowing Ted was inside, driving, watching us. I saw a tremendous roller as high as the wheelhouse, even higher, the sodium lights shining bright on its foam. It was so big, much bigger than our boat, but nothing was crashing, we were just rolling. I saw the boat go up, take the roller, then go down. I was on a tiny deck. I didn't fear I would die there, but I felt that I could so easily, that I could be extinguished and there would be nothing to account for it all. Infinite smallness is what I separated out, only a piece of this unscrupulous voyage.

A Daughter's Grand Trip

by Janice Carrillo

Final boarding call—Denver to Seville, Spain, via Chicago. Karen shouldered her dark-green backpack and adjusted the straps. A year ago, I'd accustomed myself to the idea of my only child leaving home for college in Portland, Oregon. This trip was the first step toward her required semester overseas.

Overseas? More like over a continent, over an ocean, over five or six time zones.

Her heavy nylon duffel bag was already stowed in the airplane's belly; its zipper-teeth clenched enough clothes and necessities for four months. It would have surprised neither of us if the stuffed duffel had ruptured somewhere over the Atlantic.

As she turned to say goodbye, the expression on Karen's freckled face was a medley of excitement, anticipation, and Bambi-in-the-headlights alarm. I had to keep swallowing as a fist-sized lump formed in my throat.

This wasn't the first time in Karen's life that I'd had to be a brave and selfless mother. Had I not let her finger-paint? Ride her bike to elementary school? Drive on the freeway at rush hour? This time, however, the ocean of time and space between us might span more than my heart could bear.

As the weeks passed, I began to receive postcards and, through Karen's hand, I wandered the narrow cobblestone lanes of Spain. Allowing only stingy space for address and stamp, she crowded the small cards with her precise printing.

Her host family's apartment overlooked the Guadalquivir River, which she crossed each day before walking along the Avenida de la Constitucion to her classes. Evenings out began at midnight and ended as the sun rose. Falling into bed at nine in the morning seemed natural and an afternoon siesta a necessity.

The air in Seville smelled of oranges. In a small grove of orange trees, she watched young naranjeros shake the branches, harvesting the oranges for marmalade. Hot spicy tapas simmered on wooden counters in the street cafes. With words for brush strokes, Karen painted from her exotic new palette of colors. I could taste the sizzling tapas. The tangy perfume of oranges flooded my senses.

Encouraged by the college professors, Karen and her classmates began to explore the Spanish countryside. Cordoba. La Rabida. Cadiz. Cliff houses in Ronda had stone steps leading a thousand feet to the green-and-gold valley below. Pueblos blancos were tiny whitewashed villages clinging to the steep, rocky land.

A small group of students traveled south by train to Gibraltar. After a jolting cable-car ride to the top of the Rock, they took photos of each other feeding the furry and famished Barbary apes that lived there.

On a hydrofoil, they traversed the straits for a day trip to Morocco. At the port of Tangiers, aggressive turbaned men offered themselves as guides to the young Americans, then spat at them and harassed them when the students declined.

Karen rode a camel along the windy beach and bought silver Moroccan jewelry from street vendors who smelled of pachouli oil.

On my map of Spain I circled each city she visited with a green felt-tip pen. Granada. Nerja. Malaga. Every postcard arrived with circles and arrows inked in, pointing me toward the beach she strolled at sunrise or the centuries-old bridge she crossed.

Every letter in its blue-tinted onionskin envelope drew a picture of this land of sunshine and oranges as clear as a photograph. Madrid. Toledo. Huelva. I circled the cities with my green pen. My daughter savored her surroundings.

Springtime in Seville brought Semana Santa, or Holy Week. Large platforms carrying antique gold-encrusted statues paraded through the streets, each paso held aloft by twenty hooded men. The religious festival drew huge crowds of onlookers that, Karen wrote, tumbled her along like a leaf in a river.

As I read her letter, it seemed so odd to imagine my child being jostled and bumped in that swift current of strangers participating in an ancient ritual in a foreign land.

I felt a tingle of pride in a difficult task done well, as my daughter's confidence and independent spirit bubbled from the pages I read.

I thumbed through her letters, reread the postcards stuffed edge-to-edge with minuscule handwriting, smelled the orange peel spilling from a blue-tinted envelope, and I realized how this journey benefited both of us.

I learned that I had raised a daughter willing to take risks. Karen learned she could take risks and prevail. She will draw on her Spanish experiences for a lifetime. With a keen eye for drama and beauty, she shared her experiences with me.

Through my daughter, I heard the wail of the saeta singing religious praise at Semana Santa, and felt the rough coat of a desert camel under my hands. And when I am asked, I can almost say, "I, too, have been to Spain."

Mothering the Birds

by Deborah Crooks

I'd all but forgotten about my wedding dress until I saw the box emblazoned with the words "Your Wedding Dress" sitting beneath a rusted birdcage under my house. My newly divorced husband and I had once used the cage to keep a pair of zebra finches we'd purchased shortly after our wedding. But soon after we brought the birds home, our cat launched a terrorist campaign that succeeded in giving the red, black, and white finches heart failure. Similar mishandling had left our marriage in the dust, and I had come to regard our shared home as a cage of sorts that I needed to escape.

The honeymoon had ended quickest for the dress. After the ceremony, I sent it to the dry cleaner's, where it was steamed, pressed, and impregnated with wadded-up tissue paper, then boxed so as to be rendered archival. The confection was then placed in storage so it could be passed on to future generations as a cherished keepsake.

The juxtaposition of the birdcage and the dress box was

uncanny. I'd spent many years studying birds as well as keeping them as pets. Something in them mirrored my lifelong, restless desire for freedom that I'd been unable to reconcile with the practicalities of keeping a home, an area in which my mother was a master.

I grew up in a rural area of Santa Cruz County, California, which was home to a large avian population. Quail ran through our yard at dawn, towhees pilfered from the dog dish, and I fed the scrub jays that perched in the oak trees the crusts from my peanut butter sandwiches. In the spring, red-tailed hawks called to each other as the males brought food or twigs to their potential mates. The relatively large hawks were my favorite. My father, a land surveyor, noticed my love for the animals and let me use his spotting scope so I could more closely watch the hawks when they nested in a clump of redwood trees. I ran through the trees imitating their voices, stopping on top of a small hill to raise my arms and call to the fledglings. I hoped they'd mistake me for one of them and, once, they nearly did. They flew in circles over my head, grew confused, and, much to my disappointment, flapped away.

My love for the outdoors was diametrically opposed to my mother's sensibility. Born and raised in San Francisco, she found the country setting to which her husband had moved her a constant challenge. She was used to city sidewalks, ample movie theaters, and neighbors whose voices you could hear through the walls. She found her new living situation jarring. Her kitchen window looked out onto undeveloped and forested acreage and a pothole-riddled driveway. The nearest neighbor lived in a home that was out of view, let alone earshot. The nearest movie house was ten miles away. We could count the number of cars that passed the end of our driveway each day on one hand. Nervous on the winding country roads, my mother was afraid to drive further than the closest grocery store without my father. Most of the adults my mother saw were on television, and she spent most of her days in the company of her children.

My dad's surveying job didn't pay more than what it took to feed and house four children but he didn't want my mom to take an outside job. Her solution to entertaining herself was to keep house with vigor. She adhered to a self-imposed schedule as doggedly as if she were punching a time clock and maintained fixed weekly menus for breakfasts and household duties: Mondays were for mopping the floor and French toast while Tuesdays were for cold cereal and laundry, and so on through the week. She swept the floor after every meal and dusted during TV commercials, all the while railing against the dirt and wildness that invariably found its way in.

I reveled in the unruly outdoor environment within which our house was situated. As my mother worked to keep the house dust-free, my siblings and I played in the creek or up in the hills along the deer trails. We tried to catch lizards and frogs or went fishing at the creek, hooking trout and turning them over to see their opalescent sides, before throwing them back in. We routinely brought insects, reptiles, and amphibians home to share with our family. But when my brother and I let loose a jar full of ladybugs we had collected from the flowering lupine bushes that grew on our property, my mother cried at the sight of the little red dots crawling up and over and out from the white curtains. To our delight and her dismay, we found ladybugs inside for weeks despite her efforts to eradicate them.

My mom didn't seem to mind my brother's ease in the outdoors as much as she did mine. That I was a female at home with birds and reptiles and messes ran at odds with everything she'd learned and upheld about being a woman. While I routinely came home with grass-stained clothing and tangled hair, could identify the local birds, and read books about Bigfoot and gypsies, she wore her leopard-print coat down our driveway to collect the mail, read novels set in foreign cities, and applied makeup for a day of housework.

"I'm going to have a problem with her," I heard her muttering to my aunt as I hurried to get back outside. I was not only unkempt, I ventured places she wouldn't, and, reacting to her disapproval, I stayed outside longer. I relished the fact that I was willing to go places she wouldn't dare venture.

Nonetheless, underneath my tomboy façade was a desire to be mothered, and we made occasional stabs at establishing a common ground. I encouraged her to come outside and look through the spotting scope only to be disappointed when her nearsightedness prevented her from focusing on the hawks I so loved. She took me shopping for a taffeta dress for my First Communion ceremony and beamed with approval at the sight of me looking so feminine. But the synthetic fabric itched my legs and as soon as I came home from church, I changed into a T-shirt and corduroys and ran outside rather than visit with out-of-town relatives.

Her impulse to buy me a parakeet was no doubt prompted by her desire to both keep me inside and appease my interests. She found a listing for a bird breeder in the local newspaper and broke long enough from her housework to take me on a trip down another country road, through a strawberry field to a run-down home with cages full of cooing doves on the front deck.

The breeder answered the door wearing a floral apron with birdseed-filled pockets and offered a hearty hello. Her living room was stacked with papers and books and old chenille rugs. An aviary took up the entire backyard and the ground was coated in millet and cracked sunflower seeds. I was enchanted with the environment. My mother's forced smile couldn't hide her contempt. The house was squalid but it was alive.

The sounds of squawking parakeets, finches, canaries, and a roof-high cage full of primary-colored birds made it nearly impossible for us to converse. After much debate, I selected a blue and white parakeet from among the flock.

I named the bird George and his new home became a gold cage in the corner of our dining room. It contained two yellow plastic trays for food and water, a mirror, a swinging perch, and a cuttlebone. When I let him perch on my hand, he'd get excited and give me what I would later know as a "cloacal kiss."

"Go wash your hand," Mom yelled. Equally neat, tidy, and private about bodily functions as she was about housekeeping, my mom neglected to explain that my parakeet had tried to inseminate my hand.

Inside his cage, George ran back and forth on his perch, banged his swing against the mirror, and screamed at his own reflection. At night, I covered his cage with a blanket and he shut his eyes, curling one leg up deep into his feathers before retreating into silence. During the day, I sometimes let him out so he could stretch his wings. He circled the house in haphazard fashion, brushing his wings up against the walls and bumping into furniture. He flew low, down the hallways, up toward the ceiling, then crashed into the curtains and tumbled to the windowsill.

I imagined he wanted to migrate. All birds migrate. Some fly thousands of miles to get to a new destination; others move only a few thousand feet. They're not prompted to leave by plummeting temperatures, rather by a combination of genetics and changes in light. When the days shorten, shorebirds grow agitated, bursting into short test flights in a search for the right combination of wind speed and direction. Once aloft, they fly guided by some element in their DNA, beating their wings on blind faith, taking cues from the sun and the stars, the entire globe spread out below them.

About six years after we got George, he began to develop a tumor on the right side of his throat. The growth got larger and larger but no one took the bird to the veterinarian.

"We don't have the money," Mom said, which was true.

And George's behavior didn't change much with the growth of his tumor. He sang to his mirror and he still got excited if you came near his cage. He could still fly; but now he listed to one side as he circled above the striped couch.

Around this time, my older sister was preparing to leave for college. "Eighteen years, just like that," my mom said as she folded the last of my sister's sweaters and placed it in one of the boxes lining the trunk of the family car.

It was a big deal, my sister getting into college half a state away. I was allowed to go on the five-hour trip because it was the farthest my mother had driven without my father. We drove down Highway 5, past rows and rows of fruit trees, and my sister was so excited to be moving we actually got along. When we arrived at her college, we took three trips from the car to her third-floor dorm room.

"There's a storm that's supposed to hit," Mom said as soon as we'd loaded the last box from the car. "I don't want to get caught in it or drive in the dark."

So we got back into the car, waved to my sister standing in the shade of a palm tree, and headed back north.

Just as we reached the Santa Cruz county line, the rain started. We could barely see the road through the glass, the windshield wipers unable to keep up with the pouring rain. The road narrowed as it climbed up past open fields and apple orchards to the mouth of the canyon road we called home. We drove five miles per hour for the last mile, the water on the road making a roar as it flew up and hammered the underside of the car. I could see my mother's knuckles strained on the steering wheel.

When we got home, I walked into the dining room to cover George's cage for the night. When I looked inside, I saw his blue and white-feathered body lying still on the bottom of his cage.

In the morning, I awoke to the sounds of a helicopter overhead and water running onto the cement patio. The highway we'd driven had been closed in the night due to an El Niño–induced landslide. Over the next few months, the already swollen creeks of the county doubled, then tripled in size, charting new courses through the wooded canyons.

While my mother still didn't drive too far, something changed in her after the trip to Southern California. I recognized the defiant look in her eyes each night as she rolled the spare bed into my dad's office to sleep. It was the same look I had when I ran outside to play while she ironed clothes. She knew now that she could venture places under her own power.

It hadn't occurred to me until then that my mother might want to go somewhere new and more spacious as much as the parakeet did. Sometimes, I noticed, she vacuumed so hard she left dents in the furniture.

She didn't take much with her when she finally left: her clothing, a few plates. My dad came home from work, looked around, then went to the back of the house. A few minutes later, I heard the TV go on. I sat on the couch, getting hungry, realizing there would be nothing warm on the stove.

Over the coming weeks, my father sometimes brought home a roasted chicken in a greasy bag and a loaf of white bread, which he placed on the table with a few bags of tortilla chips and granola. Sometimes my brother came in and asked if I wanted to play catch and we went out into the driveway and threw a baseball back and forth until nightfall. Mostly the house was just quiet, George's birdcage in the garage, getting rusty.

My mother eventually moved into her own place in a town not far from where my brother, father, and I lived. Though she was as free as the birds from her wifely duties, her behavior didn't radically change. She took a job in an office, still wore makeup and kept things pristine. But she didn't seem very happy, and when she did come to visit, she did what she'd always done and set about sweeping the floor or scrubbing the sink. She was free, but she didn't seem to have any wildness.

While I was relieved to be liberated from her constant supervision, I was longing to be held, to be understood and accepted. My rebellion against my mother, though, only strengthened with my newfound anger at her leaving. I was resentful toward her when she did come to visit and went further into the places I knew she wouldn't go.

One night as I lay in bed unable to sleep, I heard a plaintive and raw sound outside my window. Knowing it came from some sort of bird, I walked outside and toward the grassy field between our house and the forest. A large bird flew up from the ground, over the house, and perched on the telephone pole. I looked up at the owl. It looked down at me, blinked, then screeched and flew to perch on another tree.

I went out into the field each night, hoping to see the owls and to be seen by them. Some evenings, I lay on the dry stubble of wild grass and waited for the owls to soar over me. I felt more at home outside than I did inside. The land held me like the absent mother for whom I wouldn't admit I was yearning.

My kinship with the birds deepened the longer I spent outdoors. I felt happiest when I could tell the owls sensed my presence and didn't fly away in fright. During the day, I collected their feathers from under the places I'd seen them perch and picked up the pellets of regurgitated fur and bone that they couldn't thoroughly digest. I took them to school to show my biology teacher and we separated the small claws, insect parts, and rodent bones from the fur. Later in the year, that same teacher would write a letter facilitating my admission into the University of California, where I could continue to study birds.

For me, falcons represented the zenith of living free. Sleek, with dramatic eye markings and a sharp bill, the raptors were once native to nearly every continent and thrived in the world's open spaces—wide rivers in the heavily forested taiga and the seacoast. Partial migrants, they tended to roost together and hunt cooperatively, yet because they ate other birds, they were potentially dangerous to each other. For large parts of the year, they flew alone.

By my senior year, I was studying the captive breeding behavior of Aplomado falcons, a smaller falcon native to the grasslands of the Southwest. I observed the birds at dawn and dusk, noting what they did before mating. Mostly, the falcons would simply perch there, ignoring each other and occasionally ruffling their feathers. The sounds of the native birds singing outside would filter through the walls and the falcons would cock their heads to the sides, listening. I'd sit in the half-light with my notebook, counting minutes between mating dances. Before the female would let the male near her, he'd perform a series of bows and scrapes, culminating in a food exchange. Appeasement strategies, they were called.

During the summer break, I lived out of a tent in the Sierra Nevada Mountains in eastern California, playing surrogate parent to the falcons that were released into the wild. Our job was to feed and protect the young birds as they learned to fly and hunt on their own. Along with two other biologists, I'd rise before dawn, heading out to an observation point on a high mountain cliff, notepaper and a half-day's worth of food in hand. I wore hiking boots and fleece, carried a rifle, a radio tracking device, and binoculars.

All day we watched birds fly: Golden eagles riding thermals over the river, white-throated swifts chasing invisible insects, orange and black tanagers slicing through the trees. Though my mother was virtually absent from my life, I was immersed as deeply as I felt possible in wild earth: sleeping on granite and waking to a view of an expanse of wilderness.

As soon as their adult plumage came in, the falcons lifted their wings and took off, flying as innate to them as migration. They danced in the air, turning swiftly to chase smaller birds. If they could meet the wind at exactly the same speed and velocity, they'd hover.

Not long after returning from a release site, I went to Pinnacles National Monument with a group of rock climbers, one of whom was a man rumored to be among the best climbers on campus. He was expert in setting up ropes and protection, and I ended up as his climbing partner for the day. A week later I invited him to dinner with some friends. After salad and penne pasta with fresh tomato sauce, we passed a pint of Ben and Jerry's Heath Bar

Crunch around the table and talked about the constellations. By 11:30 P.M., he was the only guest left in the apartment. Somewhere between drying the salad bowls and wiping the counter clean we kissed, and within twenty-four hours I had fallen in love.

That summer, I was scheduled to work in Texas at an Aplomado falcon release site. I took a temporary peregrine assignment in the north part of Yosemite National Park near Lake Eleanor while I awaited departure to Texas. The plan was for me to be in Yosemite for at least a month, then fly to Texas for another season. After that, I hoped I'd find other work out in the field.

Perhaps it was genetics or changes in light. Perhaps it was my subconscious urge to finally please my mother. Though marriage seemed a faraway idea and not something for which I was particularly well suited, when my boyfriend proposed before I left for Yosemite, I said yes.

He drove me down a narrow dirt road through a forest and to the edge of Lake Eleanor, where I met the other biologist who had come to take me to camp. I set my backpack into the center of his canoe and took the helm, sitting on my knees for the paddle across the water. It was not quite summer and the forecast promised precipitation. Already, the clouds were building on the north end of the lake. When we ran aground on a small sandy point, the rain started to fall. When I stepped ashore, my leg sank up to my thigh in wet sand.

Camp was in the trees at the base of a ridge. I set up my tent while the other biologist told me about the lookout sites and the status of the falcons. There were two birds this time, not three, and every day since the birds had been released, I was told, a pair of golden eagles had tried to attack the fledglings. Just as I zipped my pack inside my tent and put my binoculars around my neck, the other attendant ran down the hill.

"I lost one. The eagles . . . " he said. He was nearly in tears.

I got up the next morning and hiked up the hill to a small ledge of granite with my gun and telemetry unit. Once again, the clouds were building and I could barely make out a falcon flying over the ridge on the other side of the lake. The signal from the bird's radio was faint and intermittent.

By noon, it was snowing. By 3:00 P.M. I couldn't see past the tops of the trees in front of me. Feeling defeated, I descended the slope to camp at dusk. We heated water and drank our soup in silence. The night was cold. By morning a thin blanket of snow covered the beach. We spent the next three days searching for the lost bird to no avail. Finally, we packed up the site and went home.

My boyfriend was exceedingly happy to see me, and my mother was delighted to hear we had become engaged. For once I was grateful to come inside to the warmth of another human. When the Aplomado release in Texas was scrapped a week later, I set about planning a wedding. Rather than working in the wilds of southeast Texas my first year out of college, I walked down the aisle wearing a high-necked dress with lace at the wrists and hem.

While my mother approved of my marriage, we still found little common ground. We'd rejected each other for so long I wasn't sure how to let her into my life. A year into my marriage, my husband and I moved half a country away from my family and set up house in a college town at the foot of the Rocky Mountains. I rarely saw my mother more than once or twice a year for six years.

On paper, my married lifestyle seemed ideal. A career as a journalist afforded me the travel I craved. And I had the reward of returning home to a loving husband who, for the most part, oversaw the workings of our home. However, mated falcons had been my model couple and they were an endangered species. The captive ones I'd observed could be dangerous to one another; the pet birds didn't live long. I wasn't sure what sort of compass was encoded in my DNA and, like George, I felt unwieldy negotiating myself between four walls. What I knew of being a wife came from my mother and my anger toward her and what she had come to represent played out its messy course in my marriage. My husband and I bought a pair of finches, adopted a cat, maintained a green lawn, and set about grooming problems similar to those our respective parents had had.

Not believing I could simultaneously study birds and be married, I gave up field biology shortly after the wedding. By the time I divorced, I no longer owned a notepad or anything resembling a telemetry unit. I simply had a white dress in a white box. When I unearthed the box from its exile under the house, empty brown hornet nests were affixed to the box-sides but all was white and virginal within. The bead and lace bodice was crumpled slightly, but otherwise unscathed. It was beautiful . . . but contained and confined.

Husbandless and emotionally motherless, I once again sought refuge outside. I threw away the white box and tossed the dress onto a high shelf in my closet. I found my hiking boots and headed for the trailhead at the end of my street. The canyon was dark, cold, and crowded with heavy pine trees save for one cottonwood tree, which glowed gold at the mouth of the canyon. Dark-eyed juncos and flickers—white of rump with translucent red wings—landed in its branches, then took off. It was fall; some birds were leaving, and some were returning home.

The trail was tattooed with the tracks of raccoon, deer, and three-toed birds. Always, there were human footprints. I imagined myself a scientist again, venturing out into the cold, trying to make order of the lives that had passed through the snow and mud each night. Even with a telemetry unit, I knew I'd only have found pieces of their stories. There are invisible tracks, scratch marks, deep grooves, and claw etchings inside of each of us.

Two nights after the full moon, I brought the wedding dress along for a hike. At the base of the gold-leafed tree, I draped the dress on a hanger and placed it in the highest branch I could reach. A cool breeze flew over the hillside, rustling the dry leaves beneath the linen. The following two weeks, the wind blew and the rain fell. Regardless of the weather, I walked past the cottonwood tree each day. The dress stayed surprisingly white and wrinkle-free as the last of the leaves fell from the tree's branches. One night, an early storm dumped thirty inches of snow. The next day someone placed the dress on a different branch.

"Never pick a live bird up by its wings," a seasoned ornithologist once warned me.

We were releasing an injured kestrel. Until then, I had considered a bird's wing invincible. I figured an appendage that propelled a small feathered body through storms, between trees, and across continents could withstand anything. Taking the bird by the ankles so that the narrow feet dangled in my palm, I threw it up like confetti, feeling for a moment its quick heartbeat and the taut muscles under its soft feathers. The bird hovered for just a half-second before it realized it was free, then opened its wings to full capacity and headed east.

November 1, the Day of the Dead, was cold and still. Even before I reached the base of the cottonwood I could see that the tree's branches were empty. I looked down the gulch, thinking I saw it on the ground, until my eyes adjusted to reveal a patch of snow.

Something changed in me with the dress's disappearance. The divorce was really final now. I felt a certain groundlessness in my spine: I was the bird now, ready to fly. But I was also tired. Returning home to get to sleep, I tossed and turned and knotted up my sheet at the foot of my bed, berating myself for never fully grasping the finer points of bedmaking. I remembered how my mother could make up a bed without leaving a crease in the spread. I started remembering all the other things she did well around the house. She could fold sheets perfectly so they unfurled in neat sections on the mattress, making it easy to securely tuck in their ends. She employed Ajax and a Brillo Pad so well she made once-grimy linoleum gleam. I remembered with a pang my resentment of her hypercleanliness and her aversion to the outdoors and my consequent rejection of all of her skills.

Despite their wide range, falcons return again and again to their native ground to nest. I realized, lying there in the dark, how terribly much I missed my mother. I wondered, for the first time, if she missed me as well.

Ritual

Abe Lincoln Fished Here

by Lin Sutherland

My mother was a fishing fanatic despite her Charleston, South Carolina, blue-blood upbringing. When she was twenty she graduated magna cum laude from the College of Charleston and left that city of history and suffocating social rules forever. With the twenty-dollar gold piece she got for the Math Prize, she bought a railroad ticket for as far west as it would get her. Austin, Texas, was $19.02 away.

There she met my father, a poet and horseman, and proceeded to have seven children—all girls. She also took up fishing, and by the time I was born, she had enough tackle, lawn chairs and fishing hats to fill a steamer trunk. To my father's horror, her favorite lure was blood bait. Bass and catfish were her prey.

Every summer it was my mother's custom to pack the seven of us into the DeSoto and drive from Austin to Charleston to visit our grandparents. We camped and fished the whole way.

Mama's preparations for the fifteen-hundred-mile trip consisted of packing the car with seven army cots, a basket of Stonewall peaches and sixteen gallons of live bait, with her tackle box and assorted rods and reels thrown in. Her idea of successful traveling was to get us all in the car without one of us sitting on the blood bait or left at a gas station. Once she'd done a head count and ascertained the security of the bait, she'd drive like A. J. Foyt until it was too dark to go any farther. This meant we were usually tired, hungry and lost on some back road in the middle of Louisiana or Mississippi when we stopped to camp.

"Stopping to camp" in our case meant suddenly swerving off the road when my mother spied a river or lake that stirred her sporting blood. She never once planned our stops like normal people do, timing themselves to arrive at a campsite or park around dusk. But this was the 1950s, when people still slept with the screen door unlocked and left the keys in the car. We felt perfectly safe at any roadside area, and we were.

The trip that brought us face to face with history was the one we took in the summer of 1958 when I was ten. It started normally enough. We had driven all day from Austin, into the dark and the Deep South. From the back seat, groggy and weary from the hours of travel, my sisters and I felt our mother wheel the car onto the shoulder and turn off the motor.

In the dim glow of our flashlights, we pulled out the army cots, set them up and sucked on leftover peach pits. We wanted to drop into a dead sleep, but as far as Mama was concerned, this was a perfect time to go fishing.

The problem was, Mama never seemed to notice that she was

the only one who ever caught anything bigger than a deck of cards. She also failed to recognize that she had borne seven girls, not seven Captain Ahabs. She lived under the illusion that everyone had the same enthusiasm as she did for sitting on rocks at waterside and waiting hours for something to steal the bait. Which of course never happened to her.

While we slouched around the camp making unintelligible grumbling noises, she unloaded the gallons of blood bait and her tackle box and got to work.

"Look at that big dark pool just under those cypress knees, honey," she said. "You just *know* there's a ten-pound bass waiting for me in there! I hope it's a stupid one." She whistled a snatch of "High Noon" as she explored her stock of lures, jigs and spoons.

Mama was very Zen about her fishing, giving it her complete concentration and ritualized observation. She examined each item in the tackle box with pleasure, murmuring to herself. She emerged from this reverie only when she decided on the right lure to use.

This night she announced, "I think I'll use my Good Luck Lure Number 242 on this baby." She glanced in my direction to see if I was watching and abruptly emitted a theatrical, diabolical laugh.

"He'll never escape my Magic Lucky Lure!" she went on. "We have ways of making fish welcome here at our little fish camp . . . no, Herr Lucky Lure?" Then, adjusting her fishing hat, she addressed the water in a tough-guy voice: "Prepare to meet your Maker, Lord Bass-ship."

And she cast perfectly into the heart of the cypress-root pool.

For her children, the enthusiasm and high drama my mother created around fishing was more intriguing than the activity itself. She was ceaselessly energetic and entertaining, and when she went up against a largemouth bass with a brain the size and density of a dust mote, it was no contest.

Fifteen minutes later she was addressing the bass in person as she cleaned it.

"I regret to inform you, Lord Bass-ship, that the inscrutable order of the universe has destined you to serve in the dual role of Main Guest and Dish at this evening's festivities. You have my deepest sympathy. On the other hand, the jig's up for everybody at one time or another, Bud. Fire up the logs, girls. Dinner just arrived."

Our second day on the road we passed trees dripping with Spanish moss, stately old homes and vast fields of cotton and snap beans. We sang and talked and Mama told fish stories. And finally, in the pitch black somewhere deep into Mississippi, she stopped the car.

"I hear running water," she announced.

We bailed out of the DeSoto and traipsed down from the road until we found a place where the ground got gravelly. We figured we were far enough from the road so we wouldn't be run over in the middle of the night, and we set up our cots in the usual manner: jammed against each other in line, so that if, during the night, one of us flopped an arm or leg out, the warm body of a sister would be felt. Sitting cross-legged on the cots, we munched Vienna sausage and Wonderbread sandwiches and watched Mama fish in the fast-running creek next to us. Then we fell asleep, exhausted.

As the dawn light began to come up, something like a gentle lapping at my side awoke me. I slowly let a foot slide over the edge of my cot. It fell into two feet of cold water. I bolted upright and saw that seven sisters and their mother were about to float away.

My mother had camped us in a creekbed. The water had risen during the night from rains upstream and had us surrounded. We practically had to swim to the car, pulling our cots behind us.

The third night found us somewhere in the mountains of Kentucky. I was never quite sure where we were at any given point on these trips, since I knew only one landmark—the tree-lined road to my grandparents' house—the finish line. But again, we had driven for hours into the night futilely looking for water. When we finally pulled off the road, the hills around us were black as midnight under a skillet. Then a slice of a quarter moon slid out from behind a cloud and delicately illuminated a rock gate in front of us.

"Oh, look!" Mama cried, "a national park."

There was an audible sigh of relief from the back seat. "Let's camp here, Mama!" we clamored urgently.

Since she had been slapping her cheeks for the last hour to stay awake, she agreed.

We cruised down a black dirt road into the parking area. Nestled nearby was the outline of a log cabin. Beyond that, the glint of water.

"See that!" Mama said excitedly. "A sleeping cabin. By some kind of lake. This is paradise."

We parked and unloaded the car, dragging our stuff into the log cabin.

It was open and empty. We could see it was very old and rudimentary, but it had a bathroom with running water. For us it was luxury quarters. We bathed and ate our dinner of kipper snacks and soda crackers, with Moon Pies for dessert. Then we snuggled into the cots that we'd fixed up in the one bare room.

Mama set off with long strides toward the water, gear in hand. The faint murmur of her voice as she conversed with her tackle box drifted through the open windows. With that and a cozy roof overhead, my sisters curled up and fell to sleep like a litter of puppies.

I picked up my rod and reel and, still in my pajamas, slipped quietly out the door. Across the damp grass I could see my mother's silhouette making casting motions. For a moment I felt the thrill of anticipation inherent in fishing: there was a fat catfish with my name on it waiting out there, I just knew it.

I joined my mother and we fished together. Just us, the water and the quarter moon. It was one of those moments that form a permanent part in the book of parent-child memories, though it was destined to be brief. Mama could practically conjure fish up to her, and sure enough, within half an hour she got a strike and brought in a fourteen-pound cat. Probably *my* Fat-Cat, I thought irritably.

"Look," she said, bending around me, her hands grasping mine as I held my rod. "Let me show you . . . " She made a deft flicking motion and suddenly my line shot across the water. The light of the moon made it look like the trail of a shooting star. It fell silently on the dark water and disappeared. "Right *there,*" she said lowly. "Hold tight to it."

She turned away and began cleaning her fish. I gripped the rod until my knuckles were white. I had a feeling for what was coming. Suddenly, the line lurched tight and my arms shot forward. I almost flew into the black water of the lake.

"It's a big one, Mama!" I yelled. "I don't think I can hold it." My feet were slipping down the bank, and the mud had oozed up to my ankles. "Mama, quick!"

She grasped me around the waist and yanked me back up the bank. The pull on the line lessened. "Now! Bring it in now!" she shouted. I reeled in as hard as I could. Suddenly the fish was right there below me, lying in shallow water. It was a big one, all right. Almost as big as Mama's.

"Good work," she said, leaning over and carefully pulling the catfish onto the bank. It slapped the wet grass angrily. I was exhausted. We took our fish back to the cabin and fell into a deep sleep.

It seemed only minutes later that sleep was penetrated by voices. Lots of voices. Suddenly, the door of the cabin burst open and sunlight and a large group of people led by a woman in a uniform flowed into the room. The uniformed person was in the middle of a speech. "And here we have the boyhood home of President Abraham Lincoln—Aagghhhh!!"

We all screamed at once. My mother, protective in her own quixotic way, leapt off the cot, her chenille bathrobe flapping, and shouted at the intruders, "Who do you think you are, bursting in on a sleeping family like this?"

The guide was struck speechless. She gathered herself with visible effort. "Ma'am, I don't know who you are, but this is Abraham Lincoln's Birthplace National Historic Park," she reported tersely. Her eyes quickly shifted sideways to take in two huge catfish lying on the floor. Though she tried to conceal it, her lips pursed with disgust. I knew right off she wasn't a fisherman.

"And his log cabin," she continued, "is not an overnight stopover for fishing expeditions. This is a restricted area with guided tours beginning at 7 A.M. and . . . "

"Oh my God, we overslept!" Mama shouted. "Pack the car, girls. We've got to get on the road!"

We lurched into a flurry of experienced cot-folding and were out the door in seconds.

"But, ma'am," the guide called at my mother's disappearing back, "You weren't supposed to sleep in here. This is Lincoln's Log Cabin. *It's a National Treasure!*"

"We treasure our night here," my mother shouted back, as she gunned the car around. "Abe wouldn't have minded."

With that we roared off in the direction of South Carolina. I saw a sign as we left: "Leaving Hodgenville, Kentucky, Abraham Lincoln's Birthplace. Ya'll Come Back."

"Not likely," my mother laughed. "A good fishing spot, but I hate to do anything twice, don't you?"

And that's how it happened that, during the summer I was ten, the course of history was changed. Unofficially, to be sure, but if there'd been a historical marker by that lake, it would now have to read ABE LINCOLN FISHED HERE . . . AND SO DID I.

My Mother's Boots

by Susan Spano

Ten years ago I spent a week walking the chalk downs of Wiltshire, a county about 75 miles west of London. It was May, and the paths I tramped were sloppy. But I was prepared, because I'd packed a pair of thirty-year-old boots my mother had produced from the bottom of a closet before I left and bestowed on me, her youngest daughter. They served me well in England, led me past ruins of Iron Age forts, took me up the mossy steps of medieval churches, and finally came home encrusted with gray Wiltshire clay.

I had no reason to summon my mother's boots to duty again until a year or so later, when I was assembling my gear for a Kentucky spelunking adventure. At the time, I was just starting to really travel, which is why that trip became an exercise in taking risks and testing my limits. On it I did a lot of things I probably shouldn't have, like climbing into caves without a flashlight and hiking alone on trails known to be sunbathing spots for poisonous snakes. I still like to get a rise out of my mother, so when I got home I told her about my adventures. She has been a worrywart for as long as I've known her, but she just smiled and said that a person can strike out in boots like hers without fear of snakebite.

After many excursions in my mother's boots, I've begun to suspect that they are magic. I never wear them without seeing inspiring sights, experiencing life and nature more deeply, and coming home changed. I can rarely say how, but more and more this is the whole reason I travel. My mother's boots are chestnut tan, Boy Scout standard issue, purchased about the time she bought a virtually identical pair for my brother, while suiting him up to win a chestful of merit badges. They are lined with wrinkles now, familiar to a certain Italian shoe repairman in the West Village of New York, who told me to throw them away two springs ago before I went for a hike along the Brittany coast. But I insisted that he sew the tongues back in, flew to France, and set off—at first barefoot in the sand north of Saint-Malo, and then trustingly shod all the way to Mont Saint-Michel. I do know how that walk changed me. I realized that there is no good reason to be cynical, eating oysters in Cancale and lying in clover above the Atlantic Ocean at the Pointe de la Varda. The world is still beautiful, if you have boots to see it from.

Back home, I called my mother and told her so. But she wanted to know something more mundane. "Are the bindings of the boots coming out? The bindings were coming out the year I didn't climb Longs."

For nearly ten summers during my childhood, my family

spent two weeks at a YMCA camp just outside the Rocky Mountain National Park in Colorado. My mother broke in her boots while hiking over the Front Range. Whenever I lace them up, that place comes back to me, especially 14,256-foot Longs Peak, the patriarch of the Front Range.

"Why didn't you make Longs?" I prod. "Dad and Johnnie did."

"Because of you," she says, and then I recall the trial and tribulation I was to her when she took me for a climb. I remember crying all the way up Deer Mountain—puny by anyone's estimation, except mine, at ten.

My mother loved the mountains and cut a dashing figure among them, a red bandanna around her neck, her hair blowing free—so unlike the woman who, back home, cooked dinners, ironed, and spent every Saturday morning at the beauty parlor. When she tried to leave me at the Y's children's program, I cried and screamed, in effect, holding her prisoner while my father and brother conquered Longs.

We talk about this, she without rancor. "I'd rather be a mother than a mountain climber," she says. But then, "I know I could have made Longs."

Indeed, she could have. She has been to places I may never see, sunk her feet in the sand around the Pyramids and touched Alaskan glaciers. A social studies teacher, she saw travel as a way of learning. Because of her, my vacations are never vacant. Places mean something, and it's up to me to find out what it is—

that's my mother's mandate. Besides being magical, her boots symbolize this.

But as a symbol, they're complex. When I climb mountains in them, I feel as if, by rights, my mother should be there, even though she's too old to do much walking now. I never could imagine making the kinds of sacrifices she made for her children, which is partly why I never had any. And she never pushed me.

I've wondered, though, what I'm missing. Could it be that life is really more about making sacrifices than reaching mountain summits? Is this what I'm to take from my mom—a woman who, in all respects, seems to me successful? Then why did she give me her boots, if not to urge me to climb on?

"We think back through our mothers if we are women," Virginia Woolf wrote.

On my fortieth birthday I climbed Longs, in my mother's boots, of course. I had a fellow hiker record my ascent with a camera, mostly for the benefit of my doubtful father and brother. When I got my pictures back, I stood in the camera shop amazed, because in the picture of me at the top, I looked so oddly like my mother. Oddly, because I'm the image of my dad. But on the top of Longs, I looked like her.

My mother's boots are one legacy I guess I won't pass on. So, maybe they are more a link than a legacy, between mother and daughter, two travelers on the same journey.

Full Monty

by Rian Connors

In the ocean, I float buoyant in swells beneath a tropical sunset. My skin awakens to mild salt water, to this light, warm floating that is the one thing I truly miss in the North, my beloved home.

I call to my sister Frances, swimming nearby, "I'm trying the half strip," and pull my swimsuit down to my waist. Ocean water caresses my chest, breasts, belly. "Good idea," she calls, imitating me. We float with the swells in twilight as the sun slips behind towering cumulus clouds, then sinks into the sea. Behind us on the empty white-sand beach, my two sons and two nieces build sand-castles. Earlier they shrieked with joy in their first warm ocean waves in years.

My youngest sister, Stef, swims out to join us. Frances quietly advises her of our submerged seminaked state. "Oh!" she says, and peels down her suit. She and I, with my children and her dog, are frequent swimming companions in the frigid lake at home. There we back float until our toes turn blue. Here, in the Pacific Ocean off Kauai, Stef turns to us and says, "I'm going for the full monty."

We agree instantly, and the three of us float in the sensuous touch of the ocean. We keep watch on the sunset, the rising darkness, and the children on shore. And on our mother, matriarch of this clan, who now enters the waves. Earlier her grandchildren, blissfully unaware of Mom's osteoporosis, begged her to bodysurf. Frances guides her through the gentle waves and out to join us. We swim together, surrounding her, the woman who invited us all on this trip to paradise in celebration of her seventy-fifth birthday.

"We're doing the full monty," I say teasingly, awaiting the reaction we daughters know so well. I am doubly rewarded, for while Mom's eyes and mouth speak the "Oh, you wicked girls." we expect, she tugs off her own suit. Now we are a discreetly ribald quartet off a peaceful dusky beach, caressed by healing waves, asking nothing more of the moment.

"Sure is warmer than the last time we did this," I say, and we howl with laughter at our memories of Chilkoot Trail in July 1996.

There, Frances was first in for a bath after four sweaty, bug-doped days backpacking. When I followed her into a mountain streamlet, my body registered disbelief in conflict with my eyes. I saw her floating there, and she was neither frozen nor dead, but my body could not believe life as an outcome of immersion in that stream. I submerged then and don't remember anything for a while. Anne, the eldest, came to the stream and stripped. Susan, the fourth, followed. Then Stef and Mom, again the instigator of the expedition, appeared at the streamside.

Mom sat on the soft low shore in her "old lady" shorts, plaid shirt, and sun hat. Stef undressed while the afternoon sun, finally free of overcast, poured sideways through the stream clearing. Our white bodies alternated with dark spruce shadows and the bright sunlight. We darted from pond to riffle, trying different spots and leaps, sandbars and logs. Our shrieks grew with the shock of in, out, and into the water, out to the cooling air. We were five Rubens nudes—mature bodies, beautiful at last after years upon years of living, lovemaking, not lovemaking, child-bearing, coming out, not child-bearing, aging, training, flexing, stretching, marathon running, head standing, accepting ourselves. So much harder than accepting each other, without whom in the hard years of our growing up we each would have died. Our hard times were forgotten, our backpacking blisters, hot spots, strains, and other wounds numbed, reduced, quieted on that sunny cold afternoon on the Chilkoot Trail.

So it is tonight as we float off Kauai, where our holiday comes to darkness. We pull suits back on underwater and rise like sirens from the sea to harbor each other, our children, and our mother in the soft tropical night.

Mortality

Starting Over

by Lisa Mitchell

We are at a public swimming pool by the beach when the tsunami swells to gargantuan height above the shore. I am at the entrance, about to leave, when I turn back and see it.

"Maaaa!" I scream.

She's still inside. She can't swim. A coil of electric wire clamps around my heart, zapping it to pounding pace. I plunge back into the trampling crowd to find her, hands scratching at my face as bodies thunder over me.

"Maaaa!" I bawl.

It is hopeless, and I awake leaden with grief.

I never expected to feel that kind of fierce, protective spirit for my mother, but since Dad died, my dreams have ached with tales of disaster ready to engulf her. I am not a mother, and probably never will be, but I have inherited the protective gene.

In a bout of altruistic intention, two months after Dad's funeral, I persuade Mum to come overseas with me. At seventy-one, backpacking is out of the question for her, so we plan to take a cruise ship up Alaska's inside passage, followed by a three-week bus tour of the Canadian Rockies.

This is her first holiday without Dad. He retired early, at fifty-seven, and there was nothing they liked better than to pack up their car and caravan and head off, sometimes for months at a time. Dad planned each day with meticulous efficiency. Mum took charge of the picnic basket that carried their morning and afternoon teas. Now I am to take his place as trip coordinator and companion.

Mum and I haven't spent a day alone together since I was ten years old. How does that happen to a mother and daughter? Back then, we knew the lay of our land; I would nag her for clothes that matched my best friends' wardrobes and she would sew new ones that barely cut it in the hip-chick stakes. Ours was an old-fashioned relationship of warm milk on sleepless nights and prayers before bedtime. Mum tolerated no nonsense and passed on a strict moral code.

It wasn't until my late teens that I discovered my father's bottle of Vodka hidden in the filing cabinet of his home office, the odorless clear spirit consuming his until, one by one, he drove friends and family away. In the two decades that followed, I became a moderately successful, burnt-out careerwoman and Mum weathered the worst of her forty-five-year marriage.

Mum tosses and turns over the prospect of our trip, as do I. One day it seems such a good idea, the next she's not sure if she is up to it. It occurs to me that she may feel too grieved, or even a little guilty, about setting off on an adventure without him, and so soon after his death. They had talked of making a trip to England, his birthplace, just before he got sick. I found the trip notes in his office. He'd made a list of places he would like to visit, written lightly on a notepad in pencil as if he knew he would never make it.

As Mum rains doubt on my best-laid plans, I fear that my wish for a bonding journey has turned into an intolerable test of endurance. A month before we leave, my partner and I break up. Then I get retrenched from my job. For me, it is a devastating string of events. I wanted a thriving relationship, not one that crumbles into indifference. And after ten solid years of wringing dry each career opportunity, I am bereft of spirit to start over. I want to be strong for Mum and not ruin our trip, but weeks of sleepless nights and accumulated stress leave no energy to pull myself together. I feel like an aimless tumbleweed, scattered in the wind.

On the plane to Vancouver, there is an empty seat between us. I know Mum is thinking the same thing I am: that seat is for Dad. Despite his looming presence, our first day goes well. Mum is chatty and excited as we window-shop cosmopolitan Robson Street and head towards Burrard Inlet to admire our cruise ship, the luxurious *MS Veendam*. Tomorrow, we set sail, but tonight we must recover from jet lag.

Good God, she snores! As a kid sleeping down the hall from my parents, I blamed Dad for the early morning din that rose and fell from their bedroom. I realize there are so many things we don't know about each other.

Each time Mum opens her suitcase, she feels compelled to rearrange its contents. I could have stuffed three of her in that thing. We had several wardrobe meetings but she overpacked anyway, convinced there'd be a man like Dad to lug her baggage at every stop. Reminding her of the truth, I knew, would only present her with another excuse not to go, and we needed this break: me from my turmoil and she from her bewildering new life at home.

Dad's death has left her more alone than she cares to be and with responsibilities she hasn't managed in some years. In the five short months since his death, both our worlds have turned upside down and, when I sat down to plan a trip for us, it seemed like the only way up was north—and almost everywhere is north of Australia.

"I just want to run away," she had said, standing in the middle of the kitchen, her expression numb. I can count the few times I have seen my mother cry, but nothing compared to this dry-eyed despair. She looked lost, her unshakeable strength of mind gone, and it frightened me. I didn't know how to comfort her, so, like a parent, I promised myself to make her world a safe and happy place again.

* * *

On the deck of the *MS Veendam,* we are about to depart for Alaska's inside passage from Vancouver. Not a shuffleboard square to spare, we bounce off each other, wriggling into our life jackets. I watch Mum fumbling.

"Bet you didn't pack one of these!" I joke.

She purses her lips. Her overstuffed suitcase isn't funny. The lifeboat drill continues but in my mind, the *Veendam* breaches, her slippery decks scattered with elderly people felled by pandemonium. I'm not used to worrying about Mum.

Later, we join the party-goers at stern to set sail and sip champagne from plastic cups. I can tell, as Mum avoids the gazes of friendly golden-anniversary couples, that she feels alone, no longer part of their crowd. We are new to it all: each other's company, having fun, experiencing the relaxed space that only two people who know each other very well can reach together. While everyone else seems to fling their cares overboard, we hold on to ours.

For me, Alaska and British Columbia have always conjured up images of barrel-chested men in red flannel shirts amidst pine-clad mountains calving into rivers of mint green. As a child, I vowed to get here someday and was surprised to learn recently that Mum shared the same dream.

I travelled this route five years ago on damp ferries along the inside passage before heading south to backpack in the Canadian

Rockies. I knew a dispirited soul could find clarity along these steam-cleaned highways, surrounded by wild animals and mountain air. I hoped the chunky log cabins and shuttered cottages and cannery workers in their gumboots with earplugs dangling around their necks might remind us of simpler times, before our futures lay open and empty of purpose. This trip, I hoped, would show us a new road.

The Dalai Lama's *The Art of Happiness* is my bedtime companion. In it, he says I must embrace the trials ahead because each provides a golden opportunity to learn patience and tolerance. Mum thinks I'm silly.

"You can't find happiness in a book," she says. "What you need is a healthy diet and a haircut."

From Ketchikan to Juneau to Sitka, I itch to show Mum my memories: Ketchikan's lopsided homes with rusting, twisted cars in front yards amid the region's profusion of early summer flowers; Juneau's enchanted forest beneath Mt. Robson; the glittering interior of Sitka's Russian Orthodox church; Mt. Edgecumb's almond icing–cone reflection in the harbor. But there is souvenir shopping to do.

As I watch our precious port time slip away, Mum trawls these tourist strips with her handbag clasped tightly under her arm. I walk on her handbag side at all times, concerned someone else will agree that her five-foot frame is an easy target. Upon return to the ship, she busies herself cramming bulky Inuit dolls and padded potholders into a suitcase already fit to split.

"What time's the first seating for dinner?" Mum looks up, harried, from her recalcitrant luggage; it's still pitching stuff to the floor.

"In about twenty minutes," I say. I've been waiting for *her* to take her shower, trying to meld into *her* routine and buffer this foreign schedule that keeps catching her by surprise. But she throws me a disapproving look, suggesting it's my fault our time has scurried away. The golden opportunities to practice patience are mounting. Her lips disappear in a tight grimace. She throws things back into the suitcase so hard the Inuit dolls squeak in protest. Worse, I am confronted with a portrait of my own temper tantrums. It appears my mother and I share more than the same face in the mirror.

The cruise company has assigned our dining table with the rigor of a dating agency: it's full of mother-daughter teams and recent widows. Over a week of dinners, Mum discovers she is not alone. Selma from Nevada lost her husband to cancer the month before we lost Dad, and Lorraine from Wisconsin lost her husband of fifty years the month after. Pat from Boston is taking a break from caring for her mother, who has dementia. (Mum nursed her mother through the same condition.) They sit across the table from each other and silently share their sadness. Like many women of their generation, they won't discuss their woes in company, but instead wear bright faces to match their conversation.

A few strained smiles and clipped comments flash around the table between mothers and daughters and it is clear to me that we daughters have misjudged the generation gap. We may be adults, but we are still our mothers' little girls, and some of our opinions, beliefs, and habits have come as a nasty surprise to them on this trip.

"Kate is far too busy to have a man in her life. She has a *career,*" Selma informs us. Daughter Kate rolls her eyes in frustration and I slip her a secret smile.

"Where's the bus into town?" Mum wants to know as we disembark at Valdez to track down more souvenirs.

"Where are you going? Why don't you ask someone first!" she demands. I don't tell her that when you've backpacked over six continents, you develop an instinct for these things.

"She always thinks she knows where she's going," Mum snickers to someone in our group.

I want to tell her that travel is the one thing that completes me: a time and place where I can be myself, away from expectations, mine and others'. But Mum hasn't met that person, who draws breath from landscapes and gains confidence from adventuring alone. To her, I am a young woman grown sullen and depressed in a demanding career, and she is frustrated by this irrational stranger-child who brightens in company but also requires long stretches of time alone to nap, think, recover.

Sipping cocktails in the Crow's Nest bar, we watch the sun set over the Pacific. It's the perfect setting for romance, but the presence of Dad or my partner, I think, would have marred this moment. The realization drags me back to melancholy. Where is our Hollywood script?

Later, finally provoked by my enduring irascible mood, Mum launches into a sour litany that lists her children's faults and misdemeanors. Blighted by our clutch of troubles, she says, we have neither the will nor strength to overcome. She is right, of course. I don't have her strength of mind, but in my efforts to bring us here, this insight is hardly the result I had hoped for.

I respond more honestly than the Dalai Lama probably thinks I should.

"I'm so sorry you feel that way. After dedicating your whole life to raising us, it must be very difficult to feel such disappointment," I go on. "After all you've sacrificed, is that what you hold on to?"

She absorbs this but says nothing. I hope I haven't hurt her. Putting myself in her shoes, I wonder if she questions her purpose now that her kids are grown. What fills the space when children and partner are gone? What is it like to start again, alone, at seventy-one? Were the years of parenting and coupling worth the loneliness she now feels? I want to ask, but I'm scared of the answer.

I didn't want my father to die. I clung to the hope he would one day express his approval of me. It took time to realize that he had expressed his love in other ways: working to send me to college, remodeling my kitchen, and panel-beating my car. In the months since my father's death, I have yearned for the wholehearted applause of my mother, wanting her to be the vocal audience Dad could not be. Silly me. As I have tried to orchestrate a healing holiday, I have become the daughter too big for her own boots and unable to fill her father's. Dad would never have left any detail of our trip to chance, like I have, or turned left, when we should have turned right.

As the days lengthen with the sun, our shroud of negativity falls away and Alaska sneaks in. The *Veendam* inches through a sea of chinking ice-coins toward the Hubbard Glacier's icy mass. A thousand birds swirl around the rocky spires of the emerald Kenai fjords. Away from the souvenir stores, Mum adores the tufted orange-beaked puffins diving for fish and the cheeky sea otters lolling about on their backs. Slowly, she is entering my world.

After our cruise, we fly back to Vancouver to join our Canadian Rockies bus tour. We meet our local hostess, Gina.

"Rule number one, people. Six, seven, eight! Up at six. Bags out at seven. Leave at eight. It's almost like a nursery rhyme, isn't it? If you say it really fast, it's easier to remember. Six-seven-eight! See?"

Gina would be better off hosting a children's television show. Her manner irritates me and many of our tour companions enormously.

"Just ignore her, darling," Mum says. "She will only spoil your trip if you allow her to."

I try to heed Mum's advice, without success.

Whistler has doubled in size since I was last here, but it still emits alpine resort charm. The scent from spruce and hemlock-lined hills purifies all inky thoughts of Gina. Mum and I separate from the group and amble about the paved village streets lined with cozy A-framed lodgings that promise shaggy thick towels and open fireplaces within. We dine at a family-style Italian restaurant where the college-boy waiter's cheerful banter eases us toward the end of a happy day. I can feel our mood shift. It feels like we're both finally letting go.

When we reach Jasper, a layer of low cloud has lifted and Mum's face beams at the sight of the spectacular peaks that flank the town. It's the first day I feel like I've had any energy to spare, and I long to walk briskly and feel my face flushed in the fresh afternoon air. As a little girl, I would skip to keep up with Mum's quick little steps. Now, we take slow ones. I want Mum to imprint this place in her memory.

In Alberta, Mum retrieves her fabled image of the Banff Springs Hotel, a mental postcard tucked away long ago. The black stone chateau presides in a stand of spruce, a likely place for kings and queens and tourists like Mum on a pilgrimage to honor childhood dreams. We explore the lamplit medieval corridors, whispering to each other in the ballroom, imagining the dancers sweeping across its polished flagstone floors. On the hotel's back terrace, we spend an entire afternoon admiring stately gardens and the lush valley view.

They are almost a mother-daughter rite of passage, these group tours of Alaska and the Rockies. We're adopted by another pair, Pat and Vicky, who snipe incessantly at each other. Mum and I trade sneaky, girlish looks at their expense. We're not doing so badly after all. At dinner with them one evening, Pat launches into a tirade against Gina, and Mum calmly offers her the same advice she offered me. Mum may not be able to control losing her husband, or resolve the troubles that plague her daughter, but she has more common sense and can-do attitude than anyone I know. Back home, before we left on this trip, I worried that she had lost that special gift.

I watch Mum's ebb turn to flow in the company of others. At the start of the trip, she'd skip lunch if I weren't around rather than dine alone. But as the days drive on, I glimpse an earlier Mum, the woman who could delight any group with her vibrant company and cry tears of laughter, not pain. I remember, now. It saddens me to think of the years she lived with my father's embittered mind and how that trampled her abiding spirit. She is repairing herself, I think.

The Trans-Canada Highway to Vancouver affords a view of majestic, snow-capped Mt. Baker, a fairytale of blanched peaks in its wake. My heart ached the last time I saw these mountains, my eyes holding on to them until they were gone. I watch Mum's eyes cling to the same peaks in a private, longing moment. For her, it grips me, these peaks will be a first and a last.

Separating at Los Angeles airport two days later, we hug each other close, crying and laughing.

"You look so small with that big backpack. I don't want to leave my little girl here," she says, pressing the last of her Canadian bills into my hand. I have another two months on the road to go.

"And I don't want to leave you alone on that long flight back to Australia," I say, slipping a pack of mints into her coat pocket.

Letting Go

by Karin Muller

Dear Mom,

I just returned from my 324th bowl of soup, the highlight of my day, and am looking forward to the 325th bowl for dinner. My underwear has several charred holes in it from trying to dry it with my hair dryer, and nothing short of a depth charge will unstop my sinuses. My bowels, on the other hand . . .

I shouldn't complain—the Hmong are all sleeping outside, wrapped in plastic with their bare feet sticking out one end. They use bricks for pillows and nestle together like spoons against the cold.

The bus clawed up the foggy mountain pass at a determined five miles per hour. We had built a protective cave of packs around Jay's outstretched leg and padded it with our much-needed jackets. The bus was crowded, and nearby passengers cast covetous glances at our spacious niche. My guilty explanations triggered an avalanche of excited questions and prodding fingers, and in the end I simply imposed myself between the new arrivals and their intended perch. One piqued passenger, less inclined to resignation than the rest, hefted the hindquarters of a full-grown pig into my lap. I let it stay.

The driver abruptly cut the engine and reversed direction, struggling to keep the bus centered on the narrow lane as we rolled backward down the hairpin turns. It took me a moment to realize that there was a fire burning between his knees. He kept going until he found a convenient place to pull over and then calmly subdued the blaze with the business end of his rubber thongs. He briefly inspected the molten wires, then released the brakes and continued his backward roll down the hill. The bus shuddered twice, reversed direction, and we were on our way again. The connection to the battery had clearly lost its life in the conflagration. Thereafter the driver simply ignored all stops that weren't positioned on a hill. Ingenious.

We rumbled into Lao Cai by early afternoon. Jay's leg had ballooned to the size of an embedded football, and the wound was red and hot to touch. We watched it carefully through three long days while I scrubbed laundry, ran down medicine and food, and ferried meals through the hotel lobby. The curious staffs were soon following me up the stairs whenever I went by. Whole gaggles of them began visiting our room several times a day to check on Jay's condition and sit down to chat with me in Vietnamese. When Jay asked me to lock the door, they calmly let themselves in with the master key, insisting that he would not recover without company to keep him in good spirits. I wilted at the thought of adding full-time hostess to my duties and thereafter clambered over the balcony, tray in hand, whenever we needed food.

The wound swelled further, all three stitches popped open, and then it began to drain. A plastic, viscous fluid flowed day and night, soaking towels and T-shirts. Eventually, tired of scrubbing homemade bandages, I tracked down sanitary napkins in the marketplace and, over Jay's objections, strapped them to his leg.

Our soup shop diet of noodles, beef broth, and the occasional egg had grown increasingly tiresome. Late one afternoon I set out on a hope-filled hunt for a few ounces of the squishy, processed cheese I had once seen for sale in faraway Hanoi.

"Cheese?" the stall owners repeated in confusion and offered me a block of tofu soaked in fish sauce.

I carefully described it to a dry goods seller: soft and eggshell white, smooth, salty, slightly sour. Made from curdled milk. I suddenly wanted some more than anything in the world.

"Curdled milk?" he repeated, his nose wrinkling well up into his eyebrows with distaste. The liquid that came out of lactating animals left to go sour?

He had a point. I bought the tofu.

The next morning I woke up with a curious feeling of anticipation, like a child on Christmas day. I had promised myself a special treat today—I was going to call home.

I spent the morning pacing restlessly around my guesthouse room. With a thirteen-hour time difference, Mom wouldn't be awake until at least 5:00 P.M. my time. The afternoon hours dragged by.

Five o'clock. My feet had already found their way to the local post office. I gave the woman behind the counter my parents' number in Virginia, then sat in one of the tiny, superheated booths while she dialed the Hanoi operator. Half an hour later no connection had been made, so I handed in a second number—a cherished friend in Boston who I hoped might come to visit me in Vietnam. Another hour passed. Finally, the main phone rang. "Boston," the woman called, "booth four."

It was Larry. "Hi," he said across the static. "Have you talked to your mom?"

Strange question. "Not yet—what's up?"

"She's had an accident."

My world went gray. It didn't spin around or get fuzzy. It just drained of all its color. "What kind of accident?" Please God, don't let it be a car.

"She fell down some stairs."

My knees turned watery with relief. She was strong and fit. The stairs at home were carpeted. A sprained ankle, some bruises, perhaps a broken leg—certainly nothing more.

"Those stone steps out in Williamsburg," Larry was saying. "It was pretty bad. She broke her collarbone and both wrists, I think, and cut her head and had some sort of seizures. I don't know if she's still in the hospital or not."

"How long's it been?"

"About three weeks."

Three weeks was forever to be in a hospital. Intensive care? She might have died and I would still be writing her letters. Three weeks. For the first time, I felt far away, inconceivably remote, a million miles from where I wanted to be. "Larry, call my folks, please. Tell them to call me here. I need to talk to them. I'll keep trying from this end."

"Will do," he said, and hung up.

The next two hours refused to pass. A month, a year, went by and still I was sitting there, waiting for the phone to ring. The post office was supposed to close at nine. At seven the woman behind the counter began to shut the doors; I was her only customer and she was bored. I begged her to stay open. I chatted with her endlessly in cheery Vietnamese. I looked at her photos of her children and told her how handsome her husband was—and all the while my mind was numb.

It just didn't make sense. I was the one trekking through the jungles, facing poachers and parasites. She was supposed to be safe at home, ready to welcome me back. It had never occurred to me that she might one day not be there. I felt utterly lost, directionless, like a kite without its string.

I had always wondered what it would be like to have a home. It was something I'd thought I'd missed out on with all the moving and family turmoil growing up. Now I knew how wrong I was. Mum was my home, my roots, the reason I could set out with confidence and explore the world. If only I could tell her. . . .

I should be home.

The phone rang. It rang! It was Mum, her voice strong and clear over the line. "I'm fine," she said gaily. "Dad says I'm always charging up and down the stairs. From now on I'm to hold the rail."

She did indeed have two broken wrists and a fractured collarbone. She had lost 15 percent of her blood through the gash on her head and had been unconscious for hours. After several days in the hospital they had let her come home, and she was recuperating under my father's care. "I'm typing all your letters now," she said, "but it's rather slow. I can only use one finger."

And at last, I started to cry.

I decided to make that last journey into the Tonkinese Alps, to finish what I had come to do. In the end I didn't stay because Mom told me to—we both knew she would be fine—I stayed because I wanted to.

Mom had always been an extraordinary influence on my life. She had taught me curiosity, passed on her restless spirit, and them sent me out into the world. I had come to Vietnam in part to fulfill her dream for me.

Her decision not to travel anymore had profoundly shaken my belief in many of the things I'd learned from her. If she no longer wanted to see the world, then what was I doing here? And then her accident, making me realize that I had a home—and that I could lose it.

But somewhere along the way I had taken over her dream and made it mine, I was ready to carry on, not in her name but in my own. I would still write letters to her daily, but in the end, I was no longer doing it for her. I was doing it for me.

Still, when I finished packing, her letters had somehow found their way into a pocket of my pack.

Two Days in Bangkok

by Bonnie Bertram

Standing on the banks of the Chao Phraya River in Bangkok, I was overwhelmed, having just arrived after twenty-one hours of traveling from New York. I downed the strongest cup of coffee I could find in the tea-dominated culture, determined to fight back jet lag and make my way to the city's Grand Palace.

I had never seen anything like Bangkok, a vast city with dome-shaped stupas of Buddhist temples rising up from the skyline. Most of the activity centered on the river and its fast-moving brackish water. Ribbons of iridescent oil shimmered in the current and the water smelled earthy and pungent from the silt and trash it carried. Even at that early hour, the air was humid and sultry. It felt smooth against my skin, but held the promise of scorching heat later in the day. The smog intensified the colors of the morning light, the scene particularly surreal because I was sharing it with my mom.

We lived on opposite coasts and hadn't seen each other for a few months, but Dad's health had gotten a lot worse in the past year and I knew Mom needed a break from her nursing duties.

They were both seventy-four years old but Dad had aged a lot more quickly than she had. When Dad got diabetes in his sixties, they had had to give up travel. For my mom, trips had been her way of asserting herself. Her travel plans were always bold, with unique and imaginative itineraries that highlighted her sophisticated view of the world.

My parents had moved from San Francisco to a beautiful, small coastal town in Northern California to raise my sister and me—a place so isolated that there wasn't a stoplight for forty miles. It wasn't a bad place to grow up, though I think that my parents, Mom especially, felt stifled and compelled to introduce my sister and me to a world beyond Gualala, California. Every summer Mom would plan one of her extensive trips while other families headed to Lake Tahoe or Disneyland. We would take the Alaska state ferry from Seattle up to Glacier Bay, or ride horses on a pack trip through Yosemite. One summer, we went to Tahiti and stayed on a scuba-diving boat; another we went to the southern hemisphere so that we could ski in New Zealand, where Mom put her Emergency Medical Technician training to work after I accidentally skied off a cliff. Recreation was not as important on these six- to eight-week trips as gaining an experience that would compensate for our rural upbringing.

Mom's sense of adventure and good health were enormous points of pride—for her and for me—and I knew that deep down she couldn't help but resent Dad's sickness.

"There's nothing golden about these years," she had said a few times on the phone, after going through the update of Dad's health problems and the doctor's reports.

I was living with my boyfriend on the East Coast and was heartbroken that I wasn't closer to home and able to help them more. Mom's sense of curiosity seemed to be slipping away and I wanted her to feel that she could still do whatever she wanted, on her own terms. She needed to feel capable and young. *I* needed her to feel capable and young. But I was nervous about how fragile she might be. I had been living away from California for so long that I had lost touch with what she could do. I wanted her to be invincible again, but given her advanced years, I knew she was more frail than I wanted to admit.

When I suggested that we take a trip together, she immediately mentioned Thailand. It was an exotic choice, but in many ways, a logical one. It would test our ability to get around a country so different from ours on our own—the language, the heat, and the culture all presented some pretty major challenges—and it was far enough away for her to feel separated from the difficulties at home. My sister volunteered to take care of Dad, and Mom asked me to plan the trip, insisting that she pay. This was new territory for me—I'd have to take my head out of the *Lonely Planet* guidebook and think more along the lines of Relais & Châteaux.

Figuring out when to cut corners and where to splurge became an interesting balancing act. I wanted to pamper Mom, but not make her feel fragile and overprotected. Would she be too tired to walk a mile in the heat of the day in Bangkok? Would an air-conditioned bus trip insult her spirit of adventure and give her the kind of trip she had spent her entire life avoiding? Would she think I was decadent and culturally insensitive if we stayed in luxurious, western hotels? How would I ensure her comfort without insulating her from authentic experiences?

Some of Mom's golf friends had been on trips hosted by Abercrombie & Kent, the upscale adventure outfitters that cater to affluent, and often older, clientele. I didn't think she was ready to resign herself to that kind of trip. So I decided we'd splurge on things that afforded us comfort and save money by trying our best to live like locals.

I'd booked a room at the posh Oriental Hotel. After taking numerous pictures of the huge bathtub and opulent marble sink, we made our way to the riverboat landing. We had told the hotel concierge we wanted to see the Grand Palace, and after we politely refused his repeated offer to get us a car, he reluctantly gave us directions to the riverboat stop and told us we needed the boat with the red flag.

I knew from Mom's visits to New York that she liked to take the subway because it made her feel like a local. While Bangkok's traffic is epic, our hotel was close to a public ferry stop on the waterway that goes through the heart of the city.

Mom walked out onto the boat landing—a floating platform that bobbed in the river—among the morning commuters and planted herself. There wasn't a railing in sight, so standing took determination. I reached out my arm to steady her but she didn't notice, perhaps intentionally. Earlier, at the airport, when I had asked if I could carry her bag, she'd scoffed, "No, why would you do that?"

A shrill whistle came from behind us. Sure enough, we had been anticipating the boat's arrival from the wrong direction. Approaching the dock quickly from the left, the boat knocked against the landing with a hard bang, receding out into the river a few feet before coming back again. Bridging the foot-wide gap separating the boat and the landing, I stepped across and turned around to give Mom a hand. A few people had wedged between us, widening the gulf, and the boat was slowly drifting back away from the dock. Panic rose up through me. Mom stood paralyzed, looking at her feet.

Finally, the boy whose job was to blow the whistle and fasten the rope across the passenger entrance held out his hand to Mom. She grabbed his forearm, took a big step, and landed on the boat.

She looked at me with a huge grin of relief and satisfaction—not only had she managed to get on the boat, but the atmosphere itself was breathtaking. Suddenly, the boat sped past the life that clung to the banks of the river—modern apartment buildings and makeshift huts on stilts. Residents were washing clothes in the river, drinking tea outside, chopping vegetables on back porches. Barges loaded with rice floated by. The children of the families living onboard played with chickens that walked freely on the boat. Dogs lazed in the sunshine atop the plastic tarp coverings. Bright cotton flags fastened to the bows of the long-tail boats waved languorously in the breeze. Simple wooden boats filled with produce moved slowly amidst the commotion, ferries chugging up and down the river narrowly missing them. It was chaos. It was mesmerizing.

"There is *no way* Susan and Bob did this," Mom said. "They did the bus tour," she said, with a trace of pride.

Bangkok buzzes with *tuk-tuks,* motorized three-wheel rickshas. Passengers sit precariously in open-air carts on cushioned plastic benches beneath metallic canopies with flashing lights, metal ornaments, and bright colors. Like tiny, energetic little gnats, they seemed emblematic of the city—a bit scary but incredibly convenient and offering a rush of excitement if you can stand it.

After a tour of the Grand Palace, we stood on the curb along a row of tour buses, drinking a bottle of cold water. To our surprise, a driver in a tuk-tuk slowed down to pick us up. Without a word, Mom ducked under the canopy, slid across the backseat and looked up at me.

"Are you up for this?" I asked.

"I don't know, but let's give it a shot," she said, hanging on to the handle that doubled as an armrest. The scooter lurched forward into a mass of traffic.

She looked across at me and smiled. The scooter engine whined and pulled us around a turn that afforded a view of the palace and vendor stalls filled with grilled bananas, coconut pudding, noodle dishes, and multicolored chili peppers.

"Can you *believe* . . . " she started. "Can you even *believe* that we're here, seeing all of this?"

Wat Pho, Bangkok's largest temple, is home to a Thai massage school, where massages are five dollars. Mom and I had spent her sixtieth birthday at a spa and considered ourselves massage connoisseurs. We weren't about to pass up this opportunity.

We were ushered into a large room, about the size of a basketball court, with raised platforms and foam mattresses in orderly rows. Clean sheets would cost an extra fifty cents. Mom was wearing an ankle-length linen dress, so a woman handed her some drawstring pants and motioned both of us to two empty mattresses.

Thai massage, it turned out, was nothing like the Swedish oil rub we were expecting. Part acupressure, part yoga, it was very physical. I couldn't help but laugh as I wondered if it was an elbow or a fork the masseuse was using on my back. Then I heard Mom laugh, too. Lying side-by-side in this foreign place, while strange women did painful things to us in the name of healing, we laughed and laughed. When it was over, Mom whispered, "They charge you five dollars for a massage but had I known, I would have given them ten dollars to leave me alone!"

Later that afternoon, while we waited at the ferry station to return to the hotel, we noticed a poster advertising "Fringe Festival," in English, with a list of upcoming events printed in Thai. Originating in Edinburgh as a showcase for up-and-coming artists, Fringe Festivals typically attract fairly bohemian crowds. I made a mental note of it as we headed back to our hotel.

Relaxing on our room's balcony, we could see a dance performance at a nearby restaurant featuring brightly colored lights and men and women in overdone traditional costumes. Row upon row of westerners ate on the floor at long tables, the dancing a backdrop for their meal. It looked dreadful. Mom didn't need to say it: That was the kind of dinner dance Susan and Bob had been to.

The next night, after getting some directions from the concierge, we made our way across the river to a district well off the beaten tourist path. Walking past an artist's welding studio, we ventured into a lush, tropical courtyard with a small amphitheater. Incense coils hanging from trees burned slowly. Traditional cha yen, tea with condensed milk, was served at a small café with rickety chairs and makeshift tables.

A local dance troupe was premiering a new show that evening at the Fringe Festival. Mom and I were among a dozen foreigners in the audience. The billed "puppet show" was anything but traditional puppetry. Each figure—made with detailed, brightly colored textiles—stood about four feet high and was operated by three dancers moving around the stage in an intricate dance. Stagehands waved long, forty-foot swaths of vibrant aquamarine silk to illustrate a stormy sea, while yellow-orange seahorse puppets bobbed in the waves. We were both spellbound.

When it was over, we followed some people to what we hoped was a taxi stand. It had been raining and the muddy streets were dotted with puddles. We walked carefully in the darkness but playfully, too, like two schoolgirls, each warning the other about the unseen holes in the road and talking endlessly about our favorite parts of the show. The night air was soft, the neighborhood quiet. There was nothing familiar about where we were: no front lawns, no sidewalks, no flickering lights from TVs in living-room windows. Just the soft sounds of people talking a gentle, foreign language and the muted light from an occasional hanging lantern. We had no idea where we were going, but we felt safe.

In those few quiet moments, walking along that road at night, there was an easiness between Mom and me that we hadn't had in years. We were relaxed, unlike our long distance phone calls where we could only catch up on what was going on in our lives, we could talk about whatever came to mind and not work off some mental list of things we needed to cover. Being together meant that we could be more like ourselves. I wasn't just the guilt-stricken far flung daughter, sad and anxious about Dad's health. And Mom was more than the thin, tired voice on the other end of the phone, speaking a strange language of medical conditions and doctor's reports. I felt re-connected to Mom in a much broader way than the crisis of Dad's health, not as someone who needed me or whom I needed, but for the person she is.

We didn't end up at a taxi stand but at one of the few restaurants in the area, overlooking the Chao Phraya River. They were closing up for the night. I went in to find someone who could call a cab for us and Mom went to the bank of the river. I was hopelessly searching for someone who could speak English when Mom called out to me.

She had found the driver of a beautiful, classic wooden boat who would take us across the river for a dime. From there, he said, we could catch a cab. The boat was elegant, like something you'd see in a glamorous Grace Kelly movie, and after boarding, I leaned back against the nautical blue canvas-upholstered seats and looked out at the night lights and at Mom, who was resting her chin on her hands, taking in the awesome beauty of the city.

Across the river, we found a taxi, and our driver, a transvestite, took us back to the Oriental Hotel. We walked through the grand, open-air lobby. Enormous wooden prayer bells hung from the ceiling. The concierge handed us each a jasmine ring, fragrant flower strands the Thai often leave as offerings, and then we headed to our room on the "women only" floor.

"My friends back home just won't believe this," Mom said. "Not a single bit of it."

Home

Afghan Journey

By Wajmah Yaqubi

The mule turned its head and tipped its ears, staring at me. I screamed. The men said to make no noise. But at the river, Mother had wailed, and I had sobbed, out of control. How could she leave us! In the end, the men hustled her aboard the raft, next to Hamid and me. In the scuffle, Mother lost her sandals. On the mule behind me, she is barefoot, her feet filthy from the dust. But she is here, thank God. Now if only the mule would stop looking at me.

The mule's haunches trembled below us, and we climbed higher. The steep, switchback trail we were climbing led to the Khyber Pass. I knew nothing of its storied history—I was just four, frightened by the dark and the mule. The air was cool, and the heady smell of spring in the mountains filled my nostrils. But I was sad. I missed my father. As the men he'd hired to smuggle us out of the country led Mother, Hamid, and me away, he looked our way, somber and forlorn. He would see us soon, he promised. Not to worry. But how was it possible not to worry? I may have been just a child, but even I knew there was cause to worry, my head crowded with memories slipping further into the past with each slumberous step of the smelly mule.

There was the big house in Kabul, the walled garden with the flowering cherry trees, one each for Hamid, me, and our two older brothers, Ahmad Wali and Abdullah. Weekends, we picnicked on the shaded lawn, my uncles in their pressed trousers lounging on the grass, my cousins and brothers vying shamelessly for their attention. Everything was so sweet! We plucked clover from the lawn, sprinkled it with salt, and ate it. Delicious!

But then came the soldiers, their voices rough and strange, and suddenly we moved. Russians, my father said. Soviets. The big house was replaced by a much smaller one. It had a tiny yard and a pink rosebush. Grapevines clung to a wood trellis. My father had planted the grapes, a vain gesture. In his heart, I know now, he had no illusion about what the future held for our family. And so it was that his hired men led us away—away from the summer home in Jalalabad where I was born—across the river, up the steep pass, under stars so close you could almost reach out and touch them. At a house somewhere, someone gave us soup, spicy and thick with rice, chicken, and vegetables. I can taste it to this day. In a ruined village, our food ran out. My mother had a boiled egg. She split it for Hamid and me, refusing any for herself. And then we were out. Pakistan, my mother said. Freedom. In Peshawar, the woman at the hotel gave us sheer chai, tea with milk and sugar. I felt better. Outside, a few days later, I saw a woman driving a car.

Now that was something. In Afghanistan, no women drove. It was unseemly. Also forbidden. This woman had red hair, curls tumbling behind her in the breeze. I looked at Hamid, and we laughed. How absurd, I thought, a woman driving a car. Afghanistan was already a memory.

From the air, it seems so barren. Bald mountains, dust-dry canyons. It's not how I remembered my country. It's not how I wanted to remember my country. Growing up, just across the Potomac River from Washington's gleaming monuments and stolid government buildings, I remember asking my mother if Afghanistan was green. "No," she replied; "it's dry as dust." For some reason, I refused to believe her. From the window of the U.N. flight to Kabul, I can see she was right.

The night before, in the Marriott Hotel in Islamabad, I asked Mother how she felt about going back. It was the first time for both of us—twenty-one years. As a photo editor, first in New York and then in Washington for *U.S. News*, I had examined thousands of images from Afghanistan over the years—photos of the Soviet occupation, of the terrible war with the mujahideen and the nightmarish shelling of Kabul. More recent images, from the Taliban era, crossed my light table all the time. My eyes bore into the pictures, willing them to yield their secrets. What was it like to live there now? How could ordinary people possibly survive? With the arrival of the Soviets, the mujahideen, and the Taliban, the gentle people I knew as a child—my handsome uncles lounging on our lawn, my coifed aunts smiling across a groaning holiday table—had been subjected to the equivalent of Dante's nine levels of hell. We knew from the odd letter home that many had died. Once when I was alone with my father in our tiny rented apartment in Virginia, he spoke obliquely about burying his brothers and sisters. We had this conversation after the heart attack that would lead to his death at age seventy-seven. Tending his siblings' gravesites, with the rest of his family so far away, my father watched as the country he loved slid ever deeper into chaos, madness, and murder.

Unspoken between Mother and me is my father's absence. How will we react to it, each of us, as we retrace his footsteps, visit the properties and businesses that were so cruelly taken from him? In the Marriott, packing our bags, I asked Mother if she was happy. "Of course, I am," she said. "I'm going to my country." On one level, communication between us is better than I could hope. Afghan tradition—and my family, in particular—eschews expressions of inner thoughts, deep emotions. Looking out the double-paned window on the final approach to Kabul, I feel many emotions melt into one—sadness, joy, hope. But mostly I am scared. What if I don't find what I'm looking for? What am I looking for? In my backpack I have a list of the places I want to visit. The houses we lived in, the cemetery where my grandfather is buried. But I'm looking for something deeper. Much as I love America, I don't feel it is where I belong. Afghanistan, I feel, is my true home. I have felt this way for as long as I can remember. It is why I am traveling on an Afghan passport. It's who I am. Suddenly, there is a rush of air, the scream of tires on asphalt. Seconds later, the plane judders to a halt. I am home.

The Kabul airport is an aviation graveyard. There are bombed and broken planes—Fokkers, ancient Boeings, Soviet helicopter gunships—bits of fuselage, carcasses of giant cargo planes, shards of engine cowling, twisted propellers. Inside the shuttered terminal, dead electrical wires hang from ruined ceiling tiles, water seeps from ruptured pipes. In the middle of a bright spring morning, it is nearly pitch dark.

I choke back tears, trying to be strong for my mother, who holds back her tears, trying to be strong for me. I clutch her hand. We move numbly outside. Beggars descend on us like flies. Many are match-thin women, filthy in tattered blue burkas. Others, men and young boys, are missing limbs or parts of limbs. Incongruously, a sweet breath of alpine air wafts over us. I inhale deeply. Soon, we are in a cab, moving our bags stacked behind us. At the hotel, more beggars, dust, chaos. A growing crowd surrounds our taxi. I am shocked, and angry. I can't believe Afghans live like this. Mother and I run upstairs, hide in our room. Before I turn the lock in the door, I am rethinking the trip. I can't do this. I want to go home! And this—the filth and bedlam in the street outside my window—this is not home.

Dinner on the hotel roof. The morning's anxiety and anger have worn off, sort of. Up here, the melee of the street is less enervating. The air is the sweetest I have ever breathed. To the northwest, the snow-capped crowns of the Paghman Range front still higher peaks of the Hindu Kush, like some fabulous opening act. To the northeast is the Shamali Plain, a once lush valley of vineyards and orchards, now laid waste by the Taliban. The former masters of Kabul had hoped that by poisoning the Shamali they would create an inhospitable wasteland between themselves and the rival Northern Alliance in the Panjshir Valley, at the far end of the great plain. They were right. They did.

On the roof of the hotel, for the first time, I feel as if I truly understand the geography of the place I have dreamed about so long from afar. Across from me at our small table, Mother's eyes shine as she points out some of the nearer landmarks. On the corner is the Malalai School my brothers Ahmad Wali and Abdullah attended before my father hurriedly packed them off to Germany, on the heels of the Soviet invasion. Just across the street is the hospital where my uncle Isah died; in his final days, my father brought Isah fresh carrot juice daily, the carrots peeled, then squeezed by a vendor on the corner of Chicken Street. My father knew these streets intimately, the shop owners, the vendors. I close my eyes and hear him laugh. I see him.

The Darul-Aman district is a moonscape. The place was named for King Amanullah, a visionary ruler widely considered the father of modern Afghanistan. Darul-Aman in its day was the locus of power and prestige in Kabul. Today, enormous craters, relics of mujahideen leader Gulbuddin Hekmatyar's relentless shelling of the city more than a decade ago, could swallow our van whole. Our driver, Khalid, weaves crazily down the Darul-Aman Road, a broad boulevard that once could have been mistaken for one of the finer avenues of Hapsburg Vienna. The poplar groves that once lined the road are all gone now. So are the houses. Mother points to piles of umber rubble. They look like giant anteater hills from a *National Geographic* special. They're all that's left of the lovely homes my aunts and uncles once lived in.

The images of my homeland the world sees today are not just heart-rending but surreal. My friends in Washington and New York, what can they possibly imagine about such a place? But I am not much different, or wasn't, until I got here. The poverty, the endless indignities in the daily struggle to survive, they're far worse than I was able to imagine before coming here. And terrible as it may seem, I am offended that Afghan people—my people—are subjected to these affronts day after day after day. The burka women, for example. They don't beg, not in the conventional sense anyway. They say prayers for me as they clutch at my head scarf. They ply me with blandishments, tell me I will have beautiful babies, tell me I am beautiful. It breaks my heart. The gulf between then and now, between my father's Afghanistan and the country I have come back to, seems impossibly wide. Mother and I walk through the crepuscular gloom of the Yellow Palace, now in ruins, and I recall the stories of my grandfather. He was King Amanullah's principal adviser. I imagine my grandfather shuttling through the palace's broad corridors on the king's business. In his place, we tread carefully, the rubble underfoot capable of concealing unexploded ordnance. The bombs and bullets have stopped flying, but no one has found the time or money to sweep the place for explosives. Few Afghans come here anyway, the ruined palace just another reminder of better days.

Like so much that was good about Afghanistan, before it was plunged into its downward spiral of misery, the Kabul Museum was the brainchild of King Amanullah, his gift to posterity. Rare manuscripts and ivories, painted ancient Roman glass, and Buddhist frescoes drew scholars and antiquities specialists from around the globe. The morning Mother and I visit, the museum is closed, but the curator, a painfully thin man in a dusty pinstriped suit, graciously agrees to give us a tour. Sadly, the only things he can show us are crate after wooden crate of shattered statues. There are pieces of what must have been beautifully carved Buddhas, some dating back centuries. Many pieces are no bigger than a fingernail. I ask the curator if the frescoes and statues can be put back together. He reaches into a box, pulls out a piece of a Buddha. It is maybe six inches long. "Nothing," he says, "is beyond repair."

Khalid stops the car at the only building still standing. Through all the hell of the past two decades, the Soviets, the mujahideen, even the deranged Taliban had not molested the small stone mausoleum where the remains of two of the prophet Mohammed's apostles lay buried. Following my mother deeper into the cemetery, I feel my hands shaking. We had heard rumors that the marble headstone on my grandfather's grave had been stolen. Would it be there? My mother says little. I feel as if I am outside my body, watching myself walk toward the headstone. It is still here. "This is your grandfather's grave." Mother's voice is quiet, unwavering. "Pray for him." I begin saying the Muslim prayers I know in my heart. When I finish, my mother points to other graves, many more than I can count. "These are your aunts, your father's sisters." Then she turns. "These are your uncles, your father's brothers." Quietly, Mother names the names I have heard for so many years. I drop to my knees, sobbing. It feels as if all these relatives had just died, right here and now. Time passes, I don't know how much. More composed, I introduce myself to my relatives. "Salaam, I am Wajmah Yaqubi, Mohammed Wali Yaqubi's daughter." I ramble on. Mother does not speak. The sun begins to vanish behind the crown of a hill. I rise to go. At the grave of the two apostles, Mother and I say a final prayer.

I miss America. The thought comes to me as I fight back tears, arguing with the dull-eyed government functionary. It is my passport—I must have been crazy to come here with Afghan travel documents. This man is talking seriously about not letting me leave. Something about an exit visa. I do not have one, and he refuses to grant one. "I guess you're just going to have to stay here in Kabul, little lady." The other government men snicker into their sleeves. I flinch, picturing myself in a burka, alone, navigating the chaos of Kabul's broken streets. I refuse to cry, but my desire for home—for my friends and my family in America—is suddenly palpable. I am confused, disappointed. Having come all this way, filled with so much hope, after all this time, I feel I have failed somehow to connect with the people here. I love the people and have great hopes for our future. But I wanted so much to belong here, and now, now I just don't know. The dull-eyed man finally relents and issues the exit visa. I study my newly stamped Afghan passport. I will have to exchange it for a new one, for an American one, when I get home.

River Camps My Mother Used to Show Me

by Constance Helmericks

Following her divorce in 1965, amateur explorer Constance Helmericks traveled down the Peace, Slave, and Mackenzie rivers by freighter canoe with her two teenage daughters, Jean and Ann, to the Arctic Ocean. She recounts their adventures that took place over two summers in Down the River North *from which this essay is excerpted.*

Our first day really on our own found us motoring down the great flood feeling the keenest interest in finding out what lay ahead and the rarest exhilaration at our own audacity in finding out.

We started traveling very late in the day, after 5 P.M. It was only then that the rain clouds lifted.

"Don't stay out on the river when it gets late in the evening," the old guide had originally instructed. "Get off the river early," he had warned. Nevertheless, I felt we could count on about four hours' light today. It was eighty miles to Peace River town. At a motor speed of twelve miles per hour and a current estimated at about the same, we ought to be able to make it there before dark, with some margin. But life on a river is not that way. Nor is life any place that way, so far as I have found.

The people at Dunvegan had told us that there was another party of canoeists on the river somewhere ahead of us.

"Nobody saw them here," was the word. "They didn't stop. Very unusual this summer, two parties now, including you. Not many care to make this trip, it seems."

Official letters, I must make clear again, had assured me months ago that the Peace River canoe trip was considered a reasonable undertaking for the experienced riverman. Here was a river! Rivers naturally all have their little ways. Anyone knows that. Officials might make recommendations that rivermen be physically fit, and that their craft should meet certain specifications in size and should preferably be powered; but officials did not interfere if citizens or noncitizens decided upon any kind of expedition here—even to swim. If a person believed he could tackle the river, he had the basic right to elect himself for this undertaking. It was somewhat like a man challenging a bull in the ring in Mexico. But on the river he would experience a good many more nuances of courage and a good many more moments of truth than the bullring offers, and his dream offered beautiful scenery rather than blood. However, the individual who sets himself up to be captain of his own boat and his own life would do well to be fully aware that the authorities usually give up their search for missing persons on the river within a period of two or three days, because they never find them here.

Thinking this over, the sheltered wobbly little person who has never before faced up to such a degree of freedom wonders if he is ready for it.

"When you go out into the North," I heard many persons say both in Canada and in Alaska, "be prepared for anything. Things can happen. You never know if you're going to be out there for a day or for a year."

Quite true. Whether you travel by boat or by small airplane, in the event of power failure or some unforeseen miscalculations, you will have vanished into that wilderness, and if the northern authorities give you up for dead, you might starve to death. At one time I had become completely at home with such risks. But I now wondered how I was going to get used to them all over again.

The danger here was not just capsizing. The danger was losing your boat and dying of exposure. My big bugaboo was that somehow when we slept ashore the canoe might get away from us, and all our things in it. To overcome this fear I got rings put into each end of the canoe, and used chains with clip snaps instead of ropes. I was afraid that ropes might fray, or a beaver or porcupine might chew them—I had had that happen, once.

But the chains which arrived turned out to be cheap, flimsy things. I had asked for an eighteen-foot length of heavy-duty chain on each end. I ended up with ten-foot chains that were lightweight, and one of the nose rings was weak and wobbled during the whole trip. That's the way things go. In our civilization many people who fix things either have no imagination or don't care. I intended, therefore, always to camp in creek mouths or in eddies out of the main current. This was theoretical. Of course it did not work out that way.

Another aspect of the bugaboo was the dropping water levels. In choosing campsites, whether up some creek mouth or along the edge of the Peace, we would have to be vigilant that our heavy boat did not get so hard aground in the mud that we could never launch it again. That might be nearly as serious as losing the canoe.

And I was alert for other kinds of boat trouble. For instance, some campers have had their canoes destroyed by bears. We would therefore always take our guns ashore when we camped, and most of the spare ammunition, in an emergency pack containing a few other things to be kept right beside or even inside the sleeping bag. Bear marauders are possible but not usual. The real reason for keeping the guns right with you is for food insurance in case the canoe escapes, leaving you stranded. You should have ammunition for a half year or so. Furthermore, the big rifle might be used to signal some passing boat, in case of emergency. Since you might be camped off the main channel, it would certainly take a rifle to reach the ears of any passerby. No voice could rise above their boat's engines, even if they happened to come close to you.

Now the little motor purred softly in regular cadence, and the green-forested Alberta hills rolled by. At last I was feasting my eyes and spirit upon green. Here were the green and blue distances so loved and longed for by the longtime wilderness dweller; the feeling of freedom, the space, the golden sunlight, the clear, pure air like wine to drink in. The children opened their senses to the spirit of an empty land.

From across the water came a muffled pumping sound.

It wasn't man-made. "I think it's the slough pumper, God bless him. The great northern bittern. Funny bird, he sounds like he's trying to pump the slough dry."

"He'll never make it, Mother," laughed Ann. "There's a lot of water here."

Jean was the sole boss of the motor. She had proven to be the one in the group who had nerves of steel as well as an aptitude for mastering mechanical monsters, for which I had little love. Our lives were in the hands of a fourteen-year-old girl, I thought. Jean got very tired and her back ached from sitting sideways all day crouched over her motor jealously with greasy hands. I sat in the bow to plot our channel, and to watch for dangers, weather, man, and beast. Ann lazed away the hours opening cans of food or drink to pass around, or snoozing under the "bearskin."

The bearskin was really just my old skunk coat. It looked exactly like a black bear. It wouldn't do for a woman explorer to wear this in the woods—she might get shot!—but I had brought it along from the States to use as a comforter in the boat and for a bed skin in camping. Spruce tips and balsam boughs may be all right as a supplement, but they can never take the place of animal robes.

We had filled the canoe up with spruce tips, and had put our entire load on top of the springy, water-resistant boughs. For three people there were three wooden slat seats. The seats were built high up out of water and mud which would collect in the canoe: one seat in the bow, with leg room, and two seats quite close together in the stern. That's the way I ordered it from the factory. The high seats enabled you to observe the water half a mile ahead or more, so that you could choose your channel and not get drawn into what you didn't want. Our load was covered with canvas.

"This is Burnt River on the map," I called to the expedition members, as we approached a river mouth.

"We want to see it," came the cry.

I realized then that I was going to have a hard time getting us to Great Slave Lake in just one summer, with people who wanted to stop and see every creek along the way. But we turned in. This was the beginning of a summer of endless creeks and rivers. What were we looking for? I couldn't tell you what I was looking for in the twelve years I wandered the North before the children were born. Looking into creeks and rivers can simply become a way of life.

We nosed into Burnt River's stagnant red algae and found ourselves floating in sudden primordial silence; the humming clouds of mosquitoes which met us sounded very loud. A few big fat raindrops pattered down, the hoods of our parkas went up and the bug lotion was passed quickly from hand to hand. This typical maneuver would be repeated a thousand times until the countering readjustment tactic to nature's tactic became second nature in living afloat in the wilderness. We took up our paddles to make our way slowly through swaths of timber that had accumulated where the Peace River in flood had backed up half a mile into the creek mouth.

As the canoe tunneled into the forest, the high-water mark was above our heads. Six feet above even the reach of our paddles, its heavy gray line cut across tree trunks and along the willow fringe. Vegetation was dead from mud. Branches and leaves were festooned with mud as snow may festoon a forest. Log jams sagged over seas of mud.

"Mud," I told the kids. "Not many people have seen a sight like this." We marveled at the pure havoc of nature.

Up the river we found a moraine of continuous boulders jamming the creek bed. Everything in this whole country was either jagged rocks or mud. There wasn't a square inch of conventional, tame, normal ground anywhere.

"I want to make camp and sleep here," insisted Ann.

"No," I said. "And that's final."

We had spent an hour of daylight exploring and marveling. Off we motored, then, out of Burnt River, and on down those moving, broad sheets of water of the skylit Peace. Ann took along several large flat rocks she had gathered.

"You know what, Mom? These rocks are what we need to make steps the next time we come ashore." I smiled tolerantly, hardly dreaming what genius this child possessed, as I allowed her to take her rock steps along in the canoe.

Presently the Peace became completely glassy, almost hypnotic, as night's clouds gathered. I recognized danger.

As the shadows settle the only sound is the gurgling of the swirling boils of the river, and the occasional sound of a distant bank caving in. The whirls and boils are golden in the light of the setting sun, the sun which rolls like a ball around the horizon during the night, dipping just below the rim of the world to set in the north. The fifty-foot whirls and boils merge and dissolve, and merge again; you watch them, fascinated. Now, later, they are turning red, brassy, copper, and at last purple and black. Now the black coils of water squirm into a million changing mirror facets. Gradually it becomes impossible to tell which waters are moving in which direction. You search for indented coves where you might get ashore, but each cove is veiled in shadow, and getting in close for a look is courting danger. The old guide had cautioned against getting swept down small, narrow side channels. In floodtime some of them might be spanned with log jams. As for telling which was island and which was mainland—well, that was not always readily possible, even in broad daylight, until you got in very close.

"We've got to get off the river," I kept saying aloud to Ann, who lay near me apprehensively, on top of the load with the bearskin.

"Mother, I'm praying," she said. "You pray, too."

"I'll pray with my eyes open," I concurred, as I continued to probe the twilight with the binoculars. Big rivers can make you religious very fast, if you aren't already.

It was nearly dark when we found Griffin Creek. At first I

thought it was an island. I couldn't be sure whether it was a boat trap with a rushing narrow channel behind the island, or a safe creek from the mainland. "Turn in, turn in," I waved to Jean, and the canoe obediently turned toward the opening. Yes, the water in the opening was quiet water. Still frozen with fear, we went right into the purple darkness.

"You see, Mom, I prayed," whispered Ann sincerely.

It was hard to believe that Ann was the same twelve-year-old who a short time ago spent her whole life studying her reflection in the mirror, worrying about keeping up with the fashions of America. Who telephoned the U.S. Weather Bureau imperiously to determine which ensemble she would wear for the day. Who used up all my nail polish, razor blades, deodorants, eye make-up, and a full can of hair spray for one week's attendance of seventh grade.

I guess it was hard to realize that I myself was the same person, too, because I was now very much without the above beauty aids, and a few dozen more. As for Ann, she had forgotten they ever existed, and I should like to contend that this is a wholesome thing for twelve-year-old girls.

Griffin Creek, like Burnt River, was full of the backed-up waters of the Peace and half-submerged logs and mud. But it was safe, and we were thankful to have it.

After Jean cut the motor we heard the sweet chirping of baby frogs in chorus. They could have been angels. Paddling up around three bends of the creek, I still had no true idea of our whereabouts, when a beaver swam across our bow and cracked the water cheerfully in the gloom. That beaver materialized like a river pilot, as though he had come just to be our guide.

As the creek rapidly narrowed to nothing, a kingfisher rattled in alarm from the weird snags overhanging our heads. He had been sleeping. There was a pervading smell of wet raw earth and mud; the place smelled the way you would think coffins and earth and graveyards ought to smell, I thought; the smell of death and decay.

"Kind of a funny place, Mother," spoke up Jean, quavering.

"A rather objectionable place, dear," I agreed with trembling voice, "but we've got to make a camp here for the night somehow."

Suddenly my gaze fastened upon an object ahead in the muddy, stagnant creek bend, just as we were pushing forward, sounding with the paddles, and the hairs on the back of my neck prickled and simply stood right on end.

The object I saw ahead was the exact shape and size of a partly buried kayak.

Poling inch by inch toward the horrid object, I was certain that we had here before us the grisly remains of one of the American canoeists who had preceded us down the river. Then, just as suddenly, the object clarified itself into a perfectly ordinary, kayak-shaped white sandbar rearing out of the mists.

I groaned audibly. "Relax, Mother!" said Jean out loud. "We'll take care of you."

I had to poke at the sandbar with my paddle to make absolutely sure. Then, we turned the canoe around, retracing our way back around the bend. Somewhere in this impossible place we must make a camp tonight. We searched up and down the stagnant cut-bank channel. The only way was to cut steps up the sheer sixteen-foot raw mud walls, and choose a place that would not cave in when we did it. Then we could pitch our tent on the grassy prairie up on top.

"We can use my rocks to make our first steps," offered Ann. We set to work stamping out steps up a traverse crack in the soft and oozy mud wall, and eventually carried all our junk up.

After some hours our little band of intrepid female explorers had accomplished the herculean task. Floundering through deep mud we got the thirty-pound tent package, the stove, the grub box, the rifles, the water bucket, and three bulky eighteen-pound sleeping bags high up on the wet but clean pasture above. Here we overlooked the depths where our canoe lay tied to small poplars. Once up on top, we tugged and hauled on the tottering tent poles, and at last hitched her fast to her stakes and to some limber willows, tying the tent fly with a neat bow knot.

"You will always find that the handiest things in life," I told my campers, "are the bow knots and large safety pins."

Of course there were a few cracks over the head with the tent poles, which had a way of collapsing; and a few yelps of rage rent the peaceful night. But the main thing is that in all these episodes, we survived.

On top we had a surprisingly cheery camp. A crackling stove

inside the tent poured out its smoke from the little stovepipe, and we drank the turgid, fishy water in a nourishing, warm prepared soup mix. The prairie grass was long and filled with water. But camping right on top of such long wet herbage can give you a good camp, for if rain comes, I told my crew, it will soak right into the porous mat and there is no runoff. But you must have not only a canvas floor tarp but plenty of fur robes and eiderdown bags. Our bags had cost one hundred and twenty dollars each and were heavy duty. They were suitable for polar winter as well as summer.

It was midnight when we rolled out the three sleeping bags; but the distant sky remained pale yellow, for it was the longest day of the year.

I spread the bearskin out under my own bag, adjusted a life preserver under my head for a pillow, and crawled into my sack. All lapsed into silence.

"Thump, thump!" came mysterious sounds, close to the tent.

Jean looked out the tent flap on her hands and knees. Was it a bear? "Thump, thump, thump."

"Mother, what's that noise?"

"It's only rabbits. It will be a good rabbit year next winter."

"Mother, can I go out with the gun?"

"Not tonight, dear. For mercy sake, I haven't had a night's sleep in weeks, can't you settle down?"

"Couldn't I shoot one to eat?"

"Well, you can try, if you like. I've never been able to see one in summer."

Jean took the .22 and went outside. You could hear the dew falling. It misted onto the tent roof and saturated the long, green prairie grass. Occasionally you could hear a breeze sigh across the tent, rattling the tin safety against the little stovepipe, a breeze that spoke of our arctic prairies up north where nothing stops the wind and there is no habitation. "If only we can do this with safety!" I thought. I wouldn't want to get them into some of the tight spots I got myself into during my early life. Someday one's luck runs out.

Out in the night Jean stood silently with the little .22 rifle, surrounded by wild primroses in full bloom—Alberta's flower—and by the lovely scattered bright field lilies which were the official flower of next-door Saskatchewan. Jean's feet were wet and cold, and she had a tendency toward bronchial pneumonia; she had been hard to raise because she was allergic. She had taken years of allergy treatments. Only modern science had kept her afflictions under control and protected her from the menace of asthma.

I worried that she might shoot through the tent, what with excitement and myopia. But she never saw a rabbit—the thumping, playful varying hare or "snowshoe rabbit" which was pounding the ground with powerful hind feet. *Lepus americanus macfarlani* is rarely visible until the leaves drop.

Jean was one of those kids you see occasionally who has no visible social life—like the *Lepus americanus* in summertime.

Living in the city most of her life, she saw the others of her species only dimly through smeared glasses; and the concrete streets she walked she saw not at all. She took refuge in some inner dream because, except for our pets and the tree she climbed, she hated where she was. She became an honor student in school but aside from that became absent mentally and emotionally. Walking across a room she stumbled into things, and frequently tables, lamps, and dishes collapsed into disaster.

She lost books and sweaters and sneakers, and you caught her reading books that were far, far beyond her age, and on every notebook cover and scrap of paper she drew beautiful pictures of idealized wilderness scenes containing animals. In her early years most of the animals were horses. She cared nothing for people her own age, or friends. Her friends were animals. Her dreams were of some beautiful place that she had never been but which some uncanny instinct in her soul informed her surely must be there, if she could but find it.

Jean remains graven for me at this moment of her development on one summer night, alone with our tent. There she is, gratefully breathing in the fresh mysterious scents, and trying, eager as a pup, to catch those elusive thumping rabbits throughout the subarctic summer night. In the Peace River summer Jean was getting the chance to be young out in nature, and it was helping her to grow into some kind of real person.

Arctic Daughter

by Jean Aspen

In the mid-'70s, twenty-two-year-old Jean Aspen, daughter of Constance Helmericks, set off with her husband to live and travel the Arctic. Her book, Arctic Daughter, *from which this essay is excerpted, describes their four-year journey living in the Alaska wilderness.*

Night had already settled upon the lands to the south as our tireless sun circled the sky, dipping into the north as evening descended. From shore came the first sigh of cool dampness as the earth awoke from its afternoon doze. We spun past high cutbanks anchored in shadow and guarded by fallen trees, "sweepers" thrashing in the current. It was no place to practice our beaching techniques. Here, close to land, we were suddenly reminded of the speed and power of the water. The dark shore seemed ominous after the innocent dazzle of the river. I squinted and rubbed my salt-crusted eyes, searching the shadows where soon we must land. I ought to have a hat, I thought irritably. Uncertainly I chewed my lower lip where the skin was already peeling. A few more days of this and I'll be fried. I had forgotten the Arctic could be so hot.

A riffle broke the surface ahead and the cutbank suddenly dropped to meet it. A cutbank is where the river is eating into the shore, leaving a raw drop. "There!" I called, pointing.

Phil turned the canoe sharply upstream before nosing in to shore. Our motor conked out in the thick silt and in slow motion we slid to a stop in shallow water. It was the end of the day and we both had dry feet. We glanced at one another and shrugged.

The medium through which our canoe would not pass was far from solid. I climbed stiffly overboard and felt the penetrating stab of boots filling with cold water. Last bubbles of air hiccuped free as together we dragged our load further aground.

"Bugs!" I had forgotten them.

"I can unpack. You start a smudge fire," Phil urged, then choked on a mosquito.

Waving my arms futilely, I snapped off twigs from the lower trunks of spruce trees for a fire. The bank was a snarl of dense trees, matted with the wreckage of spring breakup and still slippery with mud. But already plants were shooting up, pushing aside their dead in the wild summer urge to grow. I cleared a space in the underbrush and soon had a fire billowing smoke from a pile of waterlogged wood. The mosquitoes were thinning when I skidded down the short cutbank to help Phil.

"Empty the cooking things out by the fire and fetch a bucket of water," he called back as he lugged his duffel up the bank, churning through dark mud. "I'll get the rest."

I noticed that he had fastened the canoe from three separate places, apprehensive that it might get away during the night.

"Think I'll try to find us a rabbit while you start supper," Phil said.

I was staking down the tent floor in a thicket of wild roses. He joined me on his knees, pulling his pliers from their holster to nip off the thorny bushes. I could see that he was anxious to be off.

"Yes, you go ahead. I can finish pitching camp."

I felt somehow disappointed to be left with the camp chores while he went off hunting. I didn't plan this trip to be left out, I thought resentfully.

I watched him pick up my old .22 rifle, holding it comfortably in one hand. It was the same gun that my mother, little sister and I had carried to the Arctic Ocean in our canoe.

"Phil, please don't lose sight of the river. A person could really get lost in this jungle. There just aren't any landmarks."

The dank forest crowded thickly to the water's edge.

"Doesn't look much like rabbit country either, does it?"

He squatted by the fire to dig through the journal box and paused to hold up his compass. Then he repacked the box and levered the lid shut. In a moment he had disappeared.

Soon I had finished pitching camp. I stirred dinner, a horse chip-and-rice dish, before moving it onto coals away from the main fire. Then I got out the tackle box. Wouldn't it be fun, I thought as I rigged my pole, if I caught a fish while he was gone.

Away from the smoke I was again immersed in a sea of mosquitoes. Carefully I traversed the broken bank, seeking a spot to fish. None seemed promising. My first cast sank through shallow muddy water and hooked into a submerged log. I wallowed out to retrieve my lure. After a few tries I retreated to the fire.

Time dragged. I glanced at my watch. Where was that Phil? I wondered, awash with irritation and concern. Positioning another log on the blaze, I wagged to keep my body in the smoke and face free as I sifted the forest noises. Evening cool was definitely upon us now, and a damp breeze from the darkening woods crept out over the gold expanse of moving water. I watched the current, caught in its timeless song. Rivers are somehow important to me. At night I often dream of drifting down rivers, the adventure of each bend unfolding before me. I have since childhood. They are the living blood of the earth. More than just moving water, there is something grand in their presence.

I sniffed the night, listening uneasily for Phil. Surely he had sense enough to stay near the water . . . ?

My mind wandered to my fourteenth summer and canoeing the Slave River in Canada. Or was it the Mackenzie the following year? I know it wasn't the Peace. The country had this same wild look, a summertime rain forest, flooded in breakup, strangled in vegetation. The sky had been rich blue that day, piled with cotton clouds. I had wanted to hunt rabbits (I never got one that year, but I looked) and I recall my mother saying:

"Jean," (she always called me that) "don't lose sight of the river or you may never find it again."

"Okay, sure," I had answered, impatient to be gone.

"I mean it now," she insisted, peering wisely over her reading glasses and laying aside her journal and pen. "You don't know everything yet."

She remained sitting cross-legged in the moss by the smudge fire, looking up at me, a plump, middle-aged woman with red hair. It is curious how our relationship reversed that summer, my mother suddenly depending on my strength and youth and judgment.

Shooting her a look of annoyance, I had taken that same .22 (old even then) and started downstream. Over the river I noticed the thunderheads building. The going was rough along the high cutbank and soon I met massive driftwood barricades which forced me inland.

The forest had been gloomy in the hush of oppressively wet air. I followed the debris until I discovered a place to crawl over it. Here I turned back toward the river only to be checked once more. I found myself bashing through ever denser thickets. Finally I decided I would have to turn around.

But I didn't emerge on shore. A gnawing fear whispered inside me, growing with the wind that rocked the spruce tops way above my head. I was suddenly aware of the rapidly changing sky. Lightning flashed and the first big drops splattered between the trees. Could I be mixed up? I glanced about, really frightened for the first time, listening for the river. Now the wind spoke and every tree complained darkly under the burden of it. The mosquitoes had vanished. Nearby something cracked explosively before the singing air. Tears streaked my scratched cheeks as confusion gave way to terror. Slowly I rotated, and suddenly each direction looked identical.

I don't recall how long I wandered or if I prayed. Time means very little in moments like that. I only remember that first glint of open sky. Heedless of the grasping branches I scrambled forward and burst into the face of the storm. The river! Despite my backtracking, I felt certain that I was still below camp. I scurried upstream along the bank, pelted by hail and spray. But no camp came into view.

"Mother!" I bawled into the wind, pivoting in frightened indecision. "Moth . . . ther!"

As if in answer, I heard the tiny "Pop!" of a rifle out of the gray ahead. I scrambled over the last few obstacles and found myself in camp.

I hugged my mother, feeling safe and foolish.

"Come on, let's get out of the storm," she said warmly, ignoring my tears and drenched clothes. She put her arm about me and started for the tent. "I fired the 30.06 hoping you could hear it over the thunder."

And I never forgot it.

But now where was that damn Phil?

The fire glowed red in the midnight dusk. Uneasily I rose for another bundle of sticks. I listened: nothing but the faraway call of geese, the hum of insects and the muted crackle of fire sluggishly pushing smoke into the calm, moist air. What if he doesn't come back? At last the thought surfaced in a black wave. What would I do? I could never find this place again if I went for help, and what good would it do anyway? I would wait here all summer if need be, but oh, please God! bring him safely back!

I was digging out the 30.06 when Phil appeared in camp, heralded by clouds of fresh mosquitoes. He took a breath and plunged into the smoke.

"What happened?" I asked as he turned to prop the .22 against a log.

His dirty face was scratched and his hair was matted with twigs. Gently I drew my arms about his waist and he stroked my hair. For a long moment we stood there, holding to the security of each other's hand.

"Come sit down," I said at last.

"I'm sure glad I took the compass," he told me sheepishly. "There was a period of time when I was certain that the compass was wrong, but it seemed unwise to argue with it."

"Dinner is ready." I placed the pot between his feet and pried up the lid. Steam enveloped him, fogging his spare glasses a moment. I seated myself across from him and smiled mischievously.

"Let me tell you a story," I said.

Refuge

by Terry Tempest Williams

LAKE LEVEL: 4203.25′

The Bird Refuge has remained a constant. It is a landscape so familiar to me, there have been times I have felt a species long before I saw it. The long-billed curlews that foraged the grasslands seven miles outside the Refuge were trustworthy. I can count on them year after year. And when six whimbrels joined them—whimbrel entered my mind as an idea. Before I ever saw them mingling with curlews, I recognized them as a new thought in familiar country.

The birds and I share a natural history. It is a matter of rootedness, of living inside a place for so long that the mind and imagination fuse.

Maybe it's the expanse of sky above and water below that soothes my soul. Or maybe it's the anticipation of seeing something new. Whatever the magic of Bear River is—I appreciate this corner of northern Utah, where the numbers of ducks and geese I find resemble those found by early explorers.

These wetlands, emeralds around Great Salt Lake, provide critical habitat for North American waterfowl and shore-birds, supporting hundreds of thousands, even millions of individuals during spring and autumn migrations. The long-legged birds with their eyes focused down transform a seemingly sterile world into a fecund one. It is here in the marshes with the birds that I seal my relationship to Great Salt Lake.

I could never have anticipated its rise.

My mother was aware of a rise on the left side of her abdomen. I was deep in dream. This particular episode found me hiding beneath my grandmother's bed as eight black helicopters flew toward the house. I knew we were in danger.

The phone rang and everything changed.

"Good morning," I answered.

"Good morning, dear," my mother replied.

This is how my days always began. Mother and I checking in—a long extension cord on the telephone lets me talk and eat breakfast at the same time.

"You're back. So how was the river trip?" I asked, pouring myself a glass of orange juice.

"It was wonderful," she answered. "I loved the river and I loved the people. The Grand Canyon is a . . ."

There was a break in her voice. I set my glass on the counter.

She paused. "I didn't want to do this, Terry."

I think I knew what she was going to say before she said it. The same way, twelve years before, I knew something was wrong when I walked into our house after school and Mother was gone. In 1971, it had been breast cancer.

With my back against the kitchen wall, I slowly sank to the floor and stared at the yellow flowered wallpaper I had always intended to change.

"What I was going to say is that the Grand Canyon is a perfect place to heal—I've found a tumor, a fairly large mass in my lower abdomen. I was wondering if you could go with me to the hospital. John has to work. I'm scheduled for an ultrasound this afternoon."

I closed my eyes. "Of course."

Another pause.

"How long have you known about this?"

"I discovered it about a month ago."

I found myself getting angry until she answered the next obvious question.

"I needed time to live with it, to think about it—and more than anything else, I wanted to float down the Colorado River. This was the trip John and I had been dreaming about for years. I knew the days in the canyon would give me peace. And Terry, they did."

I sat on the white linoleum floor in my nightgown with my knees pulled in toward my chest, my head bowed.

"Maybe it's nothing, Mother. Maybe it's only a cyst. It could be benign, you know."

She did not answer.

"How do you feel?" I asked.

"I feel fine," she said. "But I would like to go shopping for a robe before my appointment at one."

We agreed to meet at eleven.

"I'm glad you're home." I said.

"So am I."

She hung up. The dial tone returned. I listened to the line until it became clear I had heard what I heard.

It's strange to feel change coming. It's easy to ignore. An underlying restlessness seems to accompany it like birds flocking before a storm. We go about our business with the usual alacrity, while in the pit of our stomach there is a sense of something tenuous.

These moments of peripheral perceptions are short, sharp flashes of insight we tend to discount like seeing the movement of an animal from the corner of our eye. We turn and there is nothing there. They are the strong and subtle impressions we allow to slip away.

I had been feeling fey for months.

I could not read the expression on Mother's face when she came out of X-ray. She changed into her clothes and we walked out of the hospital to the car.

"It doesn't look good," she said. "It's about the size of a grapefruit, filled with fluid. They are calling in the results to the doctor. We need to go to his office to find out what to do next."

There was little emotion in her face. This was a time for details. Pragmatism replaced sentiment.

At Krehl Smith's office, the future was drawn on an 8 ½ by 11 inch pad of yellow paper. The doctor (her obstetrician who had delivered two of her four babies) proceeded to draw the tumor in relationship to her ovaries. He stumbled over his own words, not having the adequate vocabulary to tell a patient who was also a friend that she most likely had ovarian cancer.

We got the picture. There was an awkward silence.

"So what are my options?" Mother asked.

"A hysterectomy as soon as you are ready. If it is ovarian cancer then we'll follow it up with chemotherapy and go from there . . ."

"I'll make that decision," she said.

The tears I had wanted to remain hidden splashed down on the notes I was taking, blurring the ink.

Home. The family gathered in the living room. Mother had her legs on Dad's lap. Dad had his left arm around her, his right hand rubbing her knees and thighs. My brothers, Steve, Dan, and Hank, were seated across the room. I sat on the hearth. A fire was burning, so were candles. Twelve years ago, we had been too young to see beyond our own pain; children of four, eight, twelve, and fifteen. Dad was thirty-seven, in shock from the thought of losing his wife. We did not do well. She did. Things were different now. We would do it together. We made promises that we would be here for her this time, that she would not have to carry us.

The conversation shifted to mountain climbing, the men's desire to climb the Grand Teton in the summer, then on to tales of scaling Mount Everest without oxygen—it could be done.

Mother said she would like to work in the garden if the weather cleared. We said we would all help.

"That's funny," she said. "No one has ever offered to help me before."

She then asked that we respect her decisions, that this was her body and her life, not ours, and that if the tumor was malignant, she would choose not to have chemotherapy.

We said nothing.

She went on to explain why she had waited a month before going to the doctor.

"In the long run I didn't think one month would matter. In the short run, it mattered a great deal. The heat of the sandstone penetrated my skin as I lay on the red rocks. Desert light bathed my soul. And traveling through the inner gorge of Vishnu schist, the oldest exposed rock in the West, gave me a perspective that will carry me through whatever I must face. Those days on the river were a meditation, a renewal. I found my strength in its solitude. It is with me now."

She looked at Dad, "Lava Falls, John. We've got some white water ahead."

I know the solitude my mother speaks of. It is what sustains me and protects me from my mind. It renders me fully present. I am desert. I am mountains. I am Great Salt Lake. There are other languages being spoken by wind, water, and wings. There are other lives to consider: avocets, stilts, and stones. Peace is the perspective found in patterns. When I see ring-billed gulls picking on the flesh of decaying carp, I am less afraid of death. We are no more and no less than the life that surrounds us. My fears surface in my isolation. My serenity surfaces in my solitude.

It is raining. And it seems as though it has always been raining. Every day another quilted sky rolls in and covers us with water. Rain. Rain. More rain. The Great Basin is being filled.

It isn't just the clouds' doing. The depth of snowpack in the Wasatch Mountains is the highest on record. It begins to melt, and streams you could jump over become raging rivers with no place to go. Local canyons are splitting at their seams as saturated hillsides slide.

Great Salt Lake is rising.

About 14,500 years ago, Lake Bonneville spilled over the rim of the Great Basin near Red Rock Pass in southeastern Idaho. Suddenly, the waters broke the Basin, breaching the sediments down to bedrock, releasing a flood so spectacular it is estimated the maximum discharge of water was thirty-three million cubic feet per second. This event, known today as the Bonneville Flood, dropped the lake about 350 feet, to 4740 feet. When the outlet channel was eroded to resistant rock, the lake stabilized once again and the Provo Shoreline was formed.

As the climate warmed drawing moisture from the inland sea, the lake began to shrink, until, eleven thousand years ago, it had fallen to present-day levels of about 4200 feet. This trend toward warmer and drier conditions signified the end of the Ice Age.

A millennium later, the lake rose slightly to an elevation of about 4250 feet, forming the Gilbert Shoreline, but soon receded. This marked the end of Lake Bonneville and the birth of its successor, Great Salt Lake.

As children, it was easy to accommodate the idea of Lake Bonneville. The Provo Shoreline looks like a huge bathtub ring around the Salt Lake Valley. It is a bench I know well, because we lived on it. It is the ledge that supported my neighborhood above Salt Lake City. Daily hikes in the foothills of the Wasatch yielded vast harvests of shells.

"Lake Bonneville . . ." we would say as we pocketed them. Never mind that they were the dried shells of land snails. We would sit on the benches of this ancient lake, stringing white shells into necklaces. We would look west to Great Salt Lake and imagine.

That was in 1963. I was eight years old. Great Salt Lake was a puddle, having retreated to a record low surface elevation of 4191.35′. Local papers ran headlines that read,

GREAT SALT LAKE DISAPPEARING? and INLAND SEA SHRINKS.

My mother decided Great Salt Lake was something we should see before it vanished. And so, my brothers and I, with friends from the neighborhood, boarded our red Ford station wagon and headed west.

It was a long ride past the airport, industrial complexes, and municipal dumps. It was also hot. The backs of our thighs stuck to the Naugahyde seats. Our towels were wrapped around us. We were ready to swim.

Mother pulled into the Silver Sands Beach. The smell should have been our first clue, noxious hydrogen sulphide gas rising from the brine.

"Phew!" we all complained as we walked toward the beach, brine flies following us. "Smells like rotten eggs."

"You'll get used to it," Mother said. "Now go play. See if you can float."

We were dubious at best. Our second clue should have been the fact that Mother did not bring her bathing suit, but rather chose to sit on the sand in her sunsuit with a thick novel in hand.

The ritual was always the same. Run into the lake, scream, and run back out. The salt seeped into the sores of our scraped knees and lingered. And if the stinging sensation didn't bring you to tears, the brine flies did.

We huddled around Mother; the old Saltair Pavilion was visible behind her, vibrating behind a screen of heatwaves. We begged her to take us home, pleading for dry towels. Total time at the lake: five minutes. She was unsympathetic.

"We're here for the afternoon, kids," she said, and then brought down her sunglasses a bit so we could see her eyes. "I didn't see anyone floating."

She had given us a dare. One by one, we slowly entered Great Salt Lake. Gradually, we would lean backward into the hands of the cool water and find ourselves being held by the very lake that minutes before had betrayed us. For hours we floated on our backs, imprinting on Great Basin skies. It was in these moments of childhood that Great Salt Lake flooded my psyche.

Driving home, Mother asked each of us what we thought of the lake. None of us said much. We were too preoccupied with our discomfort: sunburned and salty, we looked like red gumdrops. Our hair felt like steel wool, and we smelled. With the lake so low and salinity around 26 percent, one pound of salt to every four pounds of water (half a gallon), another hour of floating in Great Salt Lake and we might have risked being pickled and cured.

The pathologist's report defined Mother's tumor as Stage III epithelial ovarian cancer. It had metastasized to the abdominal cavity. Nevertheless, Dr. Gary Smith believes Mother has a very good chance against this type of cancer, given the treatment available. He is recommending one year of chemotherapy using the agents Cytoxan and cisplatin.

Before surgery, Mother said no chemotherapy.

Today, I walked into her room, the blinds were closed.

"Terry," she said through the darkness. "Will you help me? I told myself I would not let them poison me. But now I am afraid not to. I want to live."

I sat down by her bed.

"Perhaps you can help me visualize a river—I can imagine the chemotherapy to be a river running through me. flushing the cancer cells out. Which river, Terry?"

"How about the Colorado?" I said. It was the first time in weeks I had seen my mother smile.

LAKE LEVEL: 4204.75′

What is it about the relationship of a mother that can heal or hurt us? Her womb is the first landscape we inhabit. It is here we learn to respond—to move, to listen, to be nourished and grow. In her body we grow to be human as our tails disappear and our gills turn to lungs. Our maternal environment is perfectly safe—dark, warm, and wet. It is a residency inside the Feminine.

When we outgrow our mother's body, our cramps become her own. We move. She labors. Our body turns upside down in hers as we journey through the birth canal. She pushes in pain. We emerge, a head. She pushes one more time, and we slide out like a fish. Slapped on the back by the doctor, we breathe. The umbilical cord is cut—not at our request. Separation is immediate. A mother reclaims her body, for her own life. Not ours. Minutes old, our first death is our own birth.

Mother has completed her sixth month of chemotherapy. In some ways, it is easy to become complacent, to take life for granted all over again. I welcome this luxury. I have the feeling Mother is living in the heart of each day. I am not.

Buddha says there are two kinds of suffering: the kind that leads to more suffering and the kind that brings an end to suffering.

I recall a barn swallow who had somehow wrapped his tiny leg around the top rung of a barbed-wire fence. I was walking the dikes at Bear River. When I saw the bird, my first instinct was to stop and help. But then, I thought, no, there is nothing I can do, the swallow is going to die. But I could not leave the bird. I finally took it in my hands and unwrapped it from the wire. Its heart was racing against my fingers. The swallow had exhausted itself. I placed it among the blades of grass and sat a few feet away. With each breath, it threw back its head, until the breaths grew fainter and fainter. The tiny chest became still. Its eyes were half closed. The barn swallow was dead.

Suffering shows us what we are attached to—perhaps the umbilical cord between Mother and me has never been cut. Dying doesn't cause suffering. Resistance to dying does.

* * *

LAKE LEVEL: 4209.15′

The eastern shore of Great Salt Lake is frozen, and for as far as I can see it translates into isolation. Desolation. The fog hangs low, with little delineation between earth and sky. A few ravens. A few eagles. And the implacable wind.

Snow crystals stand on the land like the raised hackles of wolves. Broken reeds and cattails are encased in ice. Great Salt Lake has not only entered the marsh, it has taken over.

Because of the high water level and the drop in salinity, Great Salt Lake can freeze and does. The transparent ice along the lake's edge is filled with bubbles of air trapped inside like the sustained notes of a soprano.

I walk these open spaces in silence, relishing the monotony of the Refuge in winter. Perhaps I am here because of last night's dream, when I stood on the frozen lake before a kayak made of sealskin. I walked on the ice toward the boat and picked up a handful of shredded hide and guts. An old Eskimo man said, "You have much to work with." Suddenly, the kayak was stripped of its skin. It was a rib cage of willow. It was the skeleton of a fish.

I want to see it for myself, wild exposure, in January, when this desert is most severe. The lake is like steel. I wrap my alpaca shawl tight around my face until only my eyes are exposed. I must keep walking to stay warm. Even the land is frozen. There is no give beneath my feet.

I want to see the lake as Woman, as myself, in her refusal to be tamed. The State of Utah may try to dike her, divert her waters, build roads across her shores, but ultimately, it won't matter. She will survive us. I recognize her as a wilderness, raw and self-defined. Great Salt Lake strips me of contrivances and conditioning, saying, "I am not what you see. Question me. Stand by your own impressions."

We are taught not to trust our own experiences. Great Salt Lake teaches me experience is all we have.

LAKE LEVEL: 4208.40′

Mimi and Mother and I had our astrology done. It seemed like a reasonable thing to do. As Mimi said, "If it sheds light on all the confusion, why not?"

We decided to have a picnic by Great Salt Lake to discuss our charts. We sat on its edge where large boulders had been brought in to secure the shore. Each of us found our own niche in the sun. Three women: a Leo, a Pisces, a Virgo. A grandmother, mother, and daughter.

It was beautiful and it was hot. We saw six ruddy ducks, one pair of redheads, avocets and stilts, flocks of Franklin gulls, young shrikes on greasewood, and meadowlarks.

Mimi and I engaged in our birding ritual: locate, focus,

observe, and identify. After the bird flies, we pore over the field guide and debate over which species we have just seen.

Mother was amused, saying she wished she liked birds as much as we did, but she had never recovered from Alfred Hitchcock's film *The Birds*. She could see herself all too well as Tippi Hedren fleeing from the wrath of gulls, regardless of whether they were ring-billed or California.

"So what do you believe?" Mother asked.

"I believe every woman should own at least one pair of red shoes . . ." I answered.

Mother grinned, "I'm being serious."

"So am I."

"When I was a young woman with four children, I was always living ahead of myself," she said. "Everything I was doing was projected toward the future, and I was so busy, busy, busy, preparing for tomorrow, for the next week, for the next month. Then one day, it all changed. At thirty-eight years old, I found I had breast cancer. I can remember asking my doctor what I should plan for in my future. He said, 'Diane, my advice to you is to live each day as richly as you can.' As I lay in my bed after he left, I thought, will I be alive next year to take my son to first grade? Will I see my children marry? And will I know the joy of holding my grandchildren?" She looked out over the water, barefoot, her legs outstretched; a white visor held down her short, black hair. "For the first time in my life, I started to be fully present in the day I was living. I was alive.

My goals were no longer long-range plans, they were daily goals, much more meaningful to me because at the end of each day, I could evaluate what I had done."

A flock of sandpipers wheeled in front of us. "I believe that when we are fully present, we not only live well, we live well for others."

Mimi questioned her, "Why is it then, Diane, that we are so willing to give up our own authority?"

"It's easier," I interjected. "We don't have to think. The responsibility belongs to someone else. Why are we so afraid of being selfish? And why do we distract and excuse ourselves from our own creativity?"

"Same reason," Mother replied. "It's easier. We haven't figured out that time for ourselves is ultimately time for our families. You can't be constantly giving without depleting the source. Somehow, somewhere, we must replenish ourselves."

"But that's antithetical to the culture we belong to," Mimi said. "We are taught to sacrifice, support, and endure. There are other virtues I am more interested in cultivating," she said, smiling.

"I have a joke." I said. "How does a man honor a woman?"

"I don't know—" Mother answered.

"He puts her on a pedestal and then asks her to get down on it."

Mimi laughed. Mother tried not to.

"That's terrible, Terry."

"Oh, Mother, loosen up. There's nobody spying on us—unless these rocks are bugged." I picked one up and looked underneath.

"We haven't touched our astrology charts," Mimi said, pulling out hers.

Mother and I found ours. We read each other's. We had already listened to the individual taped sessions.

"I liked the part about Terry being neat and meticulous," teased Mother. "I remember standing in the middle of your bedroom when you were about thirteen years old. Everything in your closet was on the floor, art and school papers were piled high on your desk. I remember thinking, I have two choices here—I can harp on her every day of her life, making certain her room is straight—or I can close the door and preserve our relationship."

"Thank you for choosing the latter," I said. "Brooke may feel otherwise."

"The thing that struck me about your chart, Diane," said Mimi, "was the tension in your life between your need for privacy and the obligation you feel toward your family."

"And I think I have paid a price physically," Mother said. She looked out over the lake, then back to me, "Did anything surprise you about your chart, Terry?"

"I think the part that helped me the most was recognizing that I operate with three minds. Remember when she said I can look at a teacup and say, 'Isn't this lovely, notice the pink roses on the white bone china,' or 'Isn't this fascinating, consider the cup in human history,' or 'Look at this teacup, the coffee stains and chip on its rim'—What about you, Mimi?" I asked.

"At seventy-nine, what did I learn? It was more an affirmation of what I already know. I am aware of my intense curiosity, my compulsion to understand the world around me. I value intelligence. I listened hard to those traits I have to watch. I realize I am a very frank, strong personality as a Leo, but I hope I can evolve to be a Leo with wisdom—

"I believe we must do things in our lives for the right reasons, because we enjoy doing them, with no expectation of getting something back in return. Otherwise, we are constantly being disappointed." She moved her turquoise bracelet back and forth on her wrist. "So I had two sons, John and Richard, because I wanted to, not because I thought they would rescue me in old age. I got out of all social organizations and clubs in my fifties so I could spend time with my grandchildren, not because they would give something back to Jack and me later on, but because that was what I wanted to do—and I have loved doing it. Believe me, these have been selfish decisions."

Silence followed.

Mimi looked at me. "And you, Terry?"

"I believe in facing life directly, to not be afraid of risking oneself for fear of losing too much." I paused. Here was my mother standing outside the shadow of cancer and my grandmother standing inside the threshold of old age. These were the women who had seen me through birth. These were the women I would see through death.

The three of us stared out at the lake, the color of Chinese porcelain, and were hypnotized by the waves.

"How do you find refuge in change?" I asked quietly.

Mimi put her broad hand on mine. "I don't know . . ." she whispered. "You just go with it."

A killdeer landed a few feet from where we were sitting.

"Kill-deer! Kill-deer! Kill-deer!"

"What bird is that?" Mother asked.

"A killdeer," Mimi answered, picking up her binoculars.

I stood up to get a better look. All at once, it began to feign a broken wing, dragging it around the sand in a circle.

"Is it hurt?" Mother asked.

"No," I said. "We must be close to its nest. She's trying to distract us. It's a protective device."

"We're not so different," Mimi said, her silver hair shining in the sun. "Shall we go?"

As we got up to leave Mother turned to me, "I'm so glad you wore your red shoes . . ."

Brooke and I slip our red canoe into Half-Moon Bay. Great Salt Lake accepts us like a lover. We dip our wooden paddles into the icy waters and make strong, rapid strokes, north. The canoe powers gracefully ahead.

For two hours we paddle forward, toward the heart of the lake.

At the bow of the boat, I face the wind. Small waves take us up and down, up and down. The water, now bottle green, becomes a seesaw. We keep paddling.

The past seven years are with me. Mother and Mimi are present. The relationships continue—something I did not anticipate.

Flocks of pintails, mallards, and teals fly over us. There are other flocks behind them, undulating strands of birds like hieroglyphics that constantly rewrite themselves. Spring migration has begun.

We keep paddling. I have a turquoise and black shawl wrapped around me, protecting my face from the cold. This shawl is from Mexico, a gift to myself from the Day of the Dead.

Wearing my owl mask, I danced in the cobblestone streets. Bonfires lit every corner. Townsfolk circled them warming their hands. Tequila poured through the gutters. In one glance, I saw both lovers and murderers kissing and knifing each other against doors. Puppet shows were performed in the plaza as firecrackers exploded at our feet. Costumed children paraded through the village, carrying illuminated gourds as lanterns. All night long there is the relentless clamouring of bells, and the baying of dogs.

Carrying a lit candle, I entered the procession of masked individuals walking toward the cemetery. We followed the pathway of petals—marigold petals sprinkled so the Dead could follow.

The iron gates were open. Hundreds of candles were flickering as families left offerings on the graves of their kin: photographs, flowers, and food; calaveras—sugared skulls—among them. Men and women washed the blue-tiled tombs that rose from the ground like altars, while other relatives cut back the vines that obscured the names of their loved ones. There were no tears here.

A crescent moon rose above the mountains, a blood-red sickle.

"*Por qué está aquí?*" asked an old woman whose arms were wide with marigolds.

I looked up and stood. "*Mi madre está muerta.*"

She points down. "*Aqui?*"

"*No, no aquí*"—not here. I try to explain in poor Spanish. "She is buried back home, *Los Estados Unidos,* but this is a good place to remember her."

We both pause.

The woman motions me to another place in the cemetery. I follow her until she turns around. She slowly sweeps her hand across five or six graves.

"*Mi familia,*" she says smiling. "*Mi esposo, mi madre y padre, mis niños.*" Then her hand moves up as she recklessly waves to the sky. "*Muy bonito . . . este cielo arriba . . . con las nubes como las rosas . . . los Muertos estan conmigos.*" I translate her words. "Very beautiful—this sky above us . . . with clouds like roses . . . the Dead are among us."

She hands me a marigold.

"*Gracias,*" I say to her. "This is the flower my mother planted each spring."

* * *

My mind returns to the lake. Our paddling has become a meditation. We are miles from shore. In sight are four blue islands: Stansbury Island on our right, Carrigan Island to our left, and straight ahead we can see Antelope Island and Fremont.

My hands are numb. We bring in our paddles and allow ourselves to float. Brooke pulls out a thermos from his pack and pours two cups of hot chocolate. I spread cream cheese over poppyseed bagels. We eat.

There is no place on earth I would rather be. Our red canoe becomes a piece of driftwood in the current. Swirls of brine shrimp eggs cloud the water. I dip my empty cup into the lake. It fills with them, tiny pink spherical eggs. They are a mystery to me. I return them. I lean into the bow of the canoe. Brooke leans into the stern. We are balanced in the lake. For what seems like hours, we float, simply staring at the sky, watching clouds, watching birds, and breathing.

A ring-billed gull flies over us, then another. I sit up and carefully take out a pouch from my pocket, untying the leather thong that has kept the delicate contents safe. Brooke sits up and leans forward. I shake petals into his hands and then into my own. Together we sprinkle marigold petals into Great Salt Lake.

My basin of tears.

My refuge.

Acknowledgments

Like a symphony, a collective of essays is more commanding than its individual parts, and so I am indebted to the talented, courageous women who have contributed very personal—sometimes, painful—stories to this anthology. I am thrilled with the range and depth of essays these writers were willing to bring forth, and feel honored to be associated with such inspiring work.

My warm thanks to Faith Conlon and Christina Henry de Tessan at Seal Press, especially Christina, whose wise counsel guided me through book titles, essay selections, permissions, and other tedious and challenging aspects of book publishing. Lauren Whaley was a true gem, helping me locate some powerful mother-daughter stories. Once again, Cindy Ringer showed her competence and good humor in assisting me with the book's administrative aspects.

I'm deeply grateful to Bobby Model for enticing me to join him in southern Sudan, and to John O'Shea, Andy Spearman, David Shand, Laurie Timpson, and other GOAL staff for making our trip to Tuic County possible. Quite unexpectedly, the Dinka people taught me more about courage and dignity and grace in three weeks' time than I could have imagined discovering in a lifetime, especially Rehan Cyer, a truly noble man.

If it were not for Richard's unwavering dedication to his daughter, and his good-natured tolerance of my gypsy lifestyle, I would not be able to travel as freely as I do. Thank you.

Most importantly, I am blessed with Alex, an unbelievably sweet daughter who recognizes my need to wander despite its discomfort to her at times. She imparts my life with joy and significance beyond words. Though my mother doesn't share Alex's understanding of my far-flung travels, I know her concerns stem from deep love. I am fortunate to be the recipient of such devotion.

About the Contributors

MOLLY AMBRECHT ABSOLON

Molly Absolon lives with her husband, Peter, and daughter, Avery, in Lander, Wyoming. A freelance writer and former instructor for the National Outdoor Leadership School, Molly has written for *Climbing*, *Backpacker*, and *High Country News* as well as many local publications. Avery was three weeks old when she first joined her parents at the cliffs and has been accompanying them on their climbing forays ever since. Motherhood has agreed with Molly and while she continues to climb, hike, ski, and play outdoors, she is just as happy watching ants with Avery as she is pushing herself to any new outdoor extremes.

KAREN ACKLAND

Karen Ackland has written for print and online publications including *Quarterly West, Cooking Light, PIF, Salon,* and *Brain Child.* In a second career, Ackland writes marketing plans, brochures, newsletters, and other ephemera for high technology and small business clients. She and her husband live in Santa Cruz, California, where they try to spend as much time outdoors as possible. To read more from Ackland, visit her Web site at *www.karenackland.com*.

Jean Aspen

Daughter of Constance Helmericks, Jean Aspen spent four years in the late 1970s in the Alaskan wilderness with her first husband. Years later, she returned to the Arctic with her second husband, Tom Irons, and their son, Luke. Today, Aspen is a high-risk obsetrical nurse and glass artist who lives outside Tucson, Arizona with her husband and son. Apsen and Irons plan another year-long Alaskan journey in 2004.

Marcia Barinaga

Marcia Barinaga is a part-time correspondent for *Science Magazine* and part-time personal essayist, whose lifelong love of science grew out of a fascination with marine biology. When she's not facedown in the water with her mother, she may be found traipsing through remote corners of Asia with her husband, Corey. Closer to her Oakland home, she spends her free time hiking the hills of West Marin county, rowing her boat on Tomales Bay, and helping her parents tend their Sonoma Mountain vineyard and transform its Cabernet Sauvignon and Chardonnay grapes into award-winning wines.

Bonnie Bertram

Bonnie Bertram is a former producer and contributor to CNN. She has written for the *International Herald Tribune, Premiere Magazine,* the *Atlanta Journal Constitution,* and other publications and was the style editor for *Atlanta Magazine*. Her foray into the dot.com world was featured in the *Wall Street Journal.* She and her journalist husband live in New York City, where she is happy to be spending time with her young daughter. She heads home to the quiet and calm of Northern California to spend time with her mom as often as possible.

Janice Carrillo

Janice Carrillo has written essays for *Newsweek,* the *Denver Post,* and the *Christian Science Monitor,* among other publications. A native of Colorado, Carrillo spent her childhood touring that state's nooks and crannies. Today, she travels anywhere at the drop of a passport. The single parent of one offspring who is now offspringing on her own, Carrillo and her daughter, Karen, have explored the American West and the capitals of Europe together. A current endeavor of Carrillo's is the creation of a regular "Algonquin Roundtable" salon for lively discussions among fellow readers, writers, and movie lovers of Denver.

Susan Catto

Susan Catto trained for a career in journalism by earning a doctorate in eighteenth-century literature at Oxford, where her favorite "professors" included Johnson, Fielding, Richardson, and the exceptional travel writer Lady Mary Wortley Montagu. Catto is a regular contributor to the *New York Times* travel section, *TIME Canada,* and *Lucky,* and the co-author of *Live and Work in the USA and Canada* (Vacation Work Publications, 3rd edition, 2003). Although she earned triple airline miles from purchases for her recent wedding, she is content to stay home in Toronto for another month or two.

RIAN CONNORS

Rian Connors is a freelance writer who lives in northern Canada. After many years of working and living on frozen water, she is always grateful to swim in a warm ocean. She learned a love of travel and adventure from her mother, with whom she travels still, most recently to China. She prefers the outback to civilization just about anywhere, so much so that her teenaged sons now consider "camping with Mom" the height of boredom.

DEBORAH CROOKS

Writer and singer Deborah Crooks has written about arts, entertainment, sports, health, and environmental issues for a variety of print and Web publications, including *America Online, Yoga Journal, VeloNews, Northern Lights, Film/Tape World,* and the *Pacific Sun.* Her work was included in *100 Years of Bicycle Racing* (Velo Press, 1997) and *Bare Your Soul: The Thinking Girl's Guide to Enlightenment* (Seal Press, 2002). She co-founded Art Not Arms and is a member of No Limits for Women in the Arts. She lives and creates in the San Francisco Bay Area.

MARJORIE FORD

Writer and psychotherapist Marjorie Ford, who was born and raised in east Oakland, California, now thrives in Tucson, Arizona. In earlier times, she worked as a secretary to Coretta Scott King, teacher, health educator, health care manager, and university administrator. She has presented women's health information through fiction in *Loving True, Living True* (Warner) and *True to Life* (Emory University), which was honored by *Ms. Magazine* and *Mademoiselle.* She is currently at work on *Sin Eater*, an autobiographical book about healing the soul, and is in remission from a second cancer episode five years ago. She has been married for twelve years to Frank Stangel, a caring, adventurous man who has traveled with her to Bahia Kino many times. Shelley and Marjorie kayaked off the shore of the Seri Indian village near Bahia Kino during Shelley's college years. Shelley, now thirty, is a successful political organizer, wife, mother—and a delight.

Ariel Gore

Ariel Gore is Maia's mom, editor/publisher of *Hip Mama* magazine, and author of *The Hip Mama Survival Guide* (Hyperion, 1998), *The Mother Trip* (Seal Press, 2000), and her memoir, *Atlas of the Human Heart* (Seal Press, 2003). She also edited the anthology *Breeder: Real Life Stories from the New Generation of Mothers* (Seal Press, 2001), with hipmama.com producer Bee Lavender. She lives, writes, and teaches in Portland, Oregon.

Constance Helmericks

Constance Helmericks went into the Alaska bush in 1944 as a young married woman. Her life as an amateur explorer on the Yukon, Koyukuk, and other rivers is told in her book *We Live in Alaska*

(Little, Brown & Co., 1944). For two summers following her divorce, she traveled by freighter canoe with her two teenage daughters down the Peace, Slave, and Mackenzie Rivers to the Arctic Ocean, a journey she chronicled in *Down The River North* (Little, Brown & Co., 1968). The trio also made a 50,000-mile car trip through the backcountry of Australia, which Helmericks described in *Australian Adventure* (Prentice-Hall, 1971). She died in 1987 after a year's struggle with cancer. She was sixty-nine years old.

Jessica Hoffmann

Jessica Hoffmann is a freelance writer/editor from Los Angeles. She writes poetry, fiction, and non-fiction, some of which has appeared in *Other Voices, Rain Taxi Review of Books, Bitch,* and the anthology *Inhabiting the Body* (Moon Journal Press, 2002). Her mom—who escaped LA as soon as Jessica graduated from high school, citing smog, traffic, and numerous pernicious aspects of movie-town culture—currently resides in a small town in Northern California. Jessica is happily nested in her hometown, where she writes, reads, and goes to the movies as often as possible.

Beth Livermore

Beth Livermore had one goal growing up: to set foot on every continent by age thirty-five. Thanks to an obliging husband, who proposed in Morocco and honeymooned with her in the Amazon, she made it by the skin of her teeth. After a career full of hair-raising adventures—swimming with sharks, rappelling Antarctic crevasses, and eating raw fish in Honduras—she entered the most harrowing odyssey of all: motherhood. Now she, her husband, and their eighteen-month-old twins, James and Julia, live smack dab in the middle of a New Jersey hayfield, where Beth continues to write, photograph, and edit stories that emphasize science and travel. Her work has been published in dozens of national magazines, including *Natural History, Travel Holiday,* and *Smithsonian,* and she has won several awards, including a Knight Science Journalism Fellowship and a National Arts Club Scholarship. She has also produced work for Insight Guides, the Discovery Channel, the National Geographic Society, and the American Museum of Natural History.

Lisa Mitchell

Lisa earned her byline reporting in the information technology press but went on to write and edit lifestyle sections for a city newspaper. She spent a year researching for a television drama, later joining a women's magazine in dot.com land. She has traveled widely over six continents. As deadlines and pocket money allow, Lisa pants up small mountains in high places. Her favorite territories include New Zealand, Alaska, British Columbia, Colorado, Patagonia, and Tasmania. She lives in Australia and currently divides her time between writing travel features and short stories and researching for travel guidebooks.

Martha Molnar

Martha Molnar is currently a communications director at a nonprofit organization, where she supervises a variety of public relations and marketing programs as well as several in-house publications. She first honed her writing skills as a journalist with local papers and later as a regular freelance writer for the *New York Times.* A mother of three children, she lives with her husband in New York's Westchester County, where she writes, gardens, and bikes regularly.

MARY MORRIS

Mary Morris is the author of five novels, including *Acts of God* (Picador, 2000) and *The Waiting Room* (Doubleday, 1989), three collections of short stories, and three travel memoirs, including *Nothing to Declare: Memoirs of a Woman Traveling Alone* (Houghton Mifflin, 1998). She co-edited, with her husband, Larry O'Connor, *Maiden Voyage* (Vintage Books, 1993), an anthology of women's travel literature. Her numerous short stories and travel essays have appeared in such places as *The Paris Review,* the *New York Times, Travel and Leisure,* and *Vogue.* The recipient of a Guggenheim Fellowship and the Rome Prize in Literature from the American Academy of Arts and Letters, Morris teaches writing at Sarah Lawrence College and lives in Brooklyn with her husband and daughter.

KARIN MULLER

Born in Switzerland and raised in the United States, Canada, and Australia, Karin Muller is an author, filmmaker, photographer, and adventurer who set out seven years ago with a backpack and a camera to travel the world's historic highways. Her first expedition took her to the Ho Chi Minh Trail in Vietnam, an adventure that culminated in her writing *Hitchhiking Vietnam* (Globe Pequot Press, 1998) and a PBS television special of the same name. She has since traveled the Inca Road and produced an international television series, *Along the Inca Road,* for *National Geographic* along with a book published by Adventure Press. Muller recently recorded six travel pieces to be aired on the national weekly radio program, "The Savvy Traveler" and was featured on *Inside Base Camp,* a 26-part *National Geographic* television series.

Hannah Nyala

Hannah was raised on a small farm in southern Mississippi. After leaving high school and her fundamentalist Christian home, she married a fellow church member and had two children, only to be battered and stalked by their father, who also abducted the children repeatedly. While her children were missing the second time, Hannah worked as a tracker and search dog handler for the National Park Service. After she and her children were reunited, she continued to track while they lived among the Ju/'hoansi Bushmen in the Kalahari Desert of southern Africa, and eventually earned master's degrees in anthropology and U.S. history. Her memoir, *Point Last Seen* (Beacon, 1997), was made into a CBS movie of the week starring Linda Hamilton. She has also authored a novel, *Leave No Trace* (Pocket, 2002), the first in a series about search-and-rescue tracker Tally Nowata, and completed the second novel, *Cry Last Heard* (Pocket 2004). She lives in a small cottage with her husband and several very large canines and tracks whenever she gets half a chance.

Emily Prager

Emily Prager is the author of three novels, including *Roger Fishbite* (Random House, 1997), and a collection of short stories. She was previously a comedy writer and columnist for *National Lampoon* and *Penthouse.* Her *Oxygen.com* commentary was honored by the Online News Association and the Columbia University Graduate School of Journalism.

Susan Spano

Susan Spano is an award-winning staff travel writer for the *Los Angeles Times,* where her weekly Her World column appears. She originated the Frugal Traveler column for the *New York Times* and co-edited two books, *Women on Divorce: A Bedside Companion* (Harcourt, 1995) and *Men on Divorce: The Other Side of the Story* (Houghton, 1997). She lives in LA, but almost always would rather be traveling.

Lin Sutherland

Lin Sutherland is a freelance writer of twenty years, specializing in humor, adventure, travel, and people. She has been published in numerous national and international magazines, including, among others, *Field and Stream, Outdoor Photographer,* and *Woman's Day.* She lives on a horse ranch outside of Austin, Texas.

Martha Sutro

Martha Sutro and her mother began their life together in Hong Kong, where Martha was born. Since then, they have hurdled through many adventures together, including hiking mountains in the Adirondacks, exploring beaches from Georgia to Virginia, and navigating the rough and rewarding terrain of a family of boys. Martha was a high-school English teacher in Vermont and San Francisco before going to the creative writing program at the University of Montana. She currently teaches, writes, sails, and cycles in Brooklyn, New York.

Terry Tempest Williams

Terry Tempest Williams grew up within sight of the Great Salt Lake in Salt Lake City, Utah. In addition to *Refuge* (Vintage Books, 1991), she is the author of *Leap* (Pantheon, 2002), *Red: Patience and Passion in the Desert* (Pantheon, 2001), and other works, including two children's books: *The Secret Language of Snow* (Sierra Club/Pantheon, 1984) and *Between Cattails* (Little Brown, 1985). Her work has appeared in *The New Yorker, The Nation, Outside, Audubon, Orion, The Iowa Review,* and *The New England Review,* among other national and international publications. Currently, Ms. Williams serves on the advisory board of the National Parks and Conservation Association, the Nature Conservancy, and the Southern Utah Wilderness Alliance. She was recently inducted into the Rachel Carson Honor Roll and has received the National Wildlife Federation's Conservation Award for Special Achievement. Formerly naturalist-in-residence at the Utah Museum of Natural History, Ms. Williams now lives in Castle Valley, Utah, with her husband Brooke Williams.

Wajmah Yaqubi

Wajmah Yaqubi recently left *U.S. News and World Report* magazine to enter the dot.com world. She now edits photography for America Online, Inc. Although she is no longer in Afghanistan, she still maintains close ties to the Afghan community in the D.C. metropolitan area and is even closer to her mother as a result of the trip. They now live only two miles apart and speak every day. Recently married, both she and her husband work part-time to further the initiative of the U.S.-Afghan Reconstruction Council, a non-profit group her husband co-founded. The group's mission is to create a strong civil society within rural Afghan communities by providing health care, education, vocational training, strong commerce, and a modern infrastructure. To read more about US-ARC, visit *www.us-arc.org*

photo © Model/M-II Images

Wendy Knight is a freelance writer who contributes to a range of publications, including the *New York Times, Outside* magazine, the *Washington Post, Mountain Gazette,* and *Vermont Life.*

Prior to writing full-time, she ran her own communications consulting firm where she developed and implemented communication strategies for clients, including Fortune 500 companies and trade associations. She has been involved in a range of public relations projects: traditional media relations, advocacy campaigns, executive communications, event planning, and editorial services.

Her book—*Managed Care: What It Is and How It Works*—was awarded "Book of the Year" in its category by the *American Journal of Nursing* in 1998. Her health care work for clients has appeared in *The New Republic, Newsweek, Time,* and *U.S. News and World Report.*

Knight received her Bachelor of Science degree in Industrial and Labor Relations from Cornell University. She lives in an old stone farmhouse in Vermont.

Credits

Grateful acknowledgment is made for permission to include material from the following sources:

"Waiting" by Molly Ambrecht Absolon. First appeared in *Climbing Magazine* in August, 2001. Used by permission of the author.

"Wuhu Diary" from *Wuhu Diary: On Taking My Adopted Daughter Back to Her Hometown in China* by Emily Prager. Copyright © 2001 by Emily Prager. Used by permission of Random House, Inc.

"Afghan Journey" by Wajmah Yubaqi. Copyright © 2002 *US News & World Report*. Reprinted with permission.

"Letting Go" by Karin Muller from *Hitchhiking Vietnam*. Copyright © 1998 Globe Pequot Press. Reprinted with permission.

"Refuge" from *Refuge: An Unnatural History of Family and Place* by Terry Tempest Williams. Copyright © 1991 Terry Tempest Williams. Used by permission of Pantheon Books, a division of Random House, Inc.

Credits

"Minding the Gap" by Mary Morris. First appeared in *Travel & Leisure*, October 2001. Reprinted by permission of the author.

"Abe Lincoln Slept Here" from *Uncommon Waters: Women Write About Fishing* edited by Holly Morris. Copyright © 1991, 1998 by Holly Morris. Used by permission of Seal Press.

"Naming Our Canyon" from *Two in The Wild: Tales of Adventure From Friends, Mothers and Daughters* edited by Susan Fox Rogers. Copyright © 1999. Used by permission of the author.

"Arctic Daughter" from *Arctic Daughter: A Wilderness Journey*. Copyright © 1998. Used by permission of the author.

"Reconnecting On the Serengeti" by Beth Livermore. First appeared in an earlier form in *Women's Sports and Fitness*, September 1995. Used by permission of the author.

"My Mother's Boots" by Susan Spano. First appeared in *New Woman Magazine* in September, 1991. Used by permission of the author.

"River Camps My Mother Used to Show Me" from *Down the Wild River North*. Copyright © Little, Brown & Co. 1968. Also appeared in *Rivers Running Free* edited by Judith Niemi and Barbara Wieser, Seal Press, 1992. Used by permission of the author's estate.

"Beyond the Portage" by Susan Catto. First appeared in an earlier form in the *New York Times*, June 23, 2002 titled "Paddling to Her

Heritage." Copyright © the *New York Times* Company. Used with permission.

"A Daughter's Grand Trip" by Janice Carrillo. First appeared in the *Christian Science Monitor,* July 6, 1998, Vol. 90, Issue 154. Used by permission of author.

"Full Monty" by Rian Connors. First appeared in *Woven on the Wind: Women Write About Friendship in the Sagebrush West* edited by Linda Hasslestrom, Gaydell Collier, and Nancy Curtis, Houghton Mifflin, 2001. Copyright © 2001 Rian Connors. Used by permission of the author.

"Escape From Parenting" by Ariel Gore. First appeared in *Salon,* November 19, 1997. Used by permission of the author.

"Ketchup and Convertibles" by Karen Ackland. First appeared in an earlier form in *Salon,* August 10, 1999. Used by permission of the author.

"Cashing Out on the Bering Sea" by Martha Sutro. First appeared in an earlier form in *Out on The Deep Blue: Men, Women, and the Oceans They Fish* edited by Leslie Leyland Fields. St. Martin's Press, 2001. Used by permission of the author.

Note

A portion of the editor's royalities will be donated to the southern Sudan relief efforts of GOAL (*www.goal.ie*), a Dublin-based international humanitarian organization that works to alleviate suffering in the developing world. GOAL operates twelve health clinics across southern Sudan that offer basic primary care services to the various tribal people in the region who have been greatly affected by the long-standing civil war. GOAL also operates basic feeding centers, builds schools, conducts immunization campaigns, and provides other humanitarian assistance.

photo © Model/M-II Images

Selected titles fro

The Unsavvy Traveler: Women's Comic Tales of Catastrophe edited by Rosemary Caperton, Anne Mathews, and Lucie Ocenas. $15.95, 1-58005-058-1. Twenty-five gut-wrenchingly funny responses to the question: What happens when trips go wrong?

A Woman Alone: Travel Tales from Around the Globe edited by Faith Conlon, Ingrid Emerick, and Christina Henry de Tessan. $15.95, 1-58005-059-X. A collection of rousing stories by women who travel solo.

Give Me the World by Leila Hadley. $14.95, 1-58005-091-3. The spirited story of one young woman's travels by boat and by land with her six-year-old son.

Solo: On Her Own Adventure edited by Susan Fox Rogers. $12.95, 1-878067-74-5. Each contributor describes the inspiring challenges and exhilarating rewards of going it alone in the outdoors.

East Toward Dawn: A Woman's Solo Journey Around the World by Nan Watkins. $14.95, 1-58005-064-6. After the loss of her son and the end of a marriage, the author sets out in search of joy and renewal in travel.

Gift of the Wild: A Woman's Book of Adventure edited by Faith Conlon, Ingrid Emerick, and Jennie Goode. $16.95, 1-58005-006-9. Explores the transformative power of outdoor adventure in the lives of women.

The Curve of Time: The Classic Memoir of a Woman and Her Children Who Explored the Coastal Waters of the Pacific Northwest, second edition by M. Wylie Blanchet, foreword by Timothy Egan. $15.95, 1-58005-072-7. The timeless memoir of a pioneering, courageous woman who acted as both mother and captain of the twenty-five foot boat that became her family's home during the long Northwest summers.

Girl in the Curl by Andrea Gabbard. $29.95, 1-58005-048-4. The first illustrated history of women surfers, *Girl in the Curl* captures an important and overlooked part of the sport's past in gorgeous color photos.

Seal Press publishes many outdoor and travel books by women writers. Please visit our website at www.sealpress.com.